WESTLAND

The Journal of John Hillary, Emigrant to
New Zealand 1879

Michael Etches and J. Haddon Hillary

Grosvenor House
Publishing Limited

All rights reserved
Copyright © Michael Etches and J. Haddon Hillary, 2025

The right of Michael Etches and J. Haddon Hillary to be
identified as the author of this
work has been asserted in accordance with Section 78
of the Copyright, Designs and Patents Act 1988

The book cover is copyright to Michael Etches and J. Haddon Hillary

This book is published by
Grosvenor House Publishing Ltd
Link House
140 The Broadway, Tolworth, Surrey, KT6 7HT.
www.grosvenorhousepublishing.co.uk

This book is sold subject to the conditions that it shall not, by way of
trade or otherwise, be lent, resold, hired out or otherwise circulated
without the author's or publisher's prior consent in any form of
binding or cover other than that in which it is published and
without a similar condition including this condition being
imposed on the subsequent purchaser.

A CIP record for this book
is available from the British Library

ISBN 978-1-83615-381-8

To Elisabeth, who introduced me to the
Hillary family

CONTENTS

Introduction	vii
Chapter 1 – Emigration	1
Chapter 2 – The "Westland"	6
Chapter 3 – The Promised Land	49
Chapter 4 – Homeward Bound	61
Chapter 5 – The Aftermath	89
Chapter 6 – Summing Up	108
Photographs	110

INTRODUCTION

In May 1990, I married Elisabeth Loney, a lady I had worked with for about four years. She was a divorcee who lived in Ipswich with her two teenage daughters, Miranda and Victoria. After our marriage, we moved into a home in Worcester Park, Surrey, and soon Liz, as she was known, gave birth to two more children, both boys whom we named Anthony and Benjamin.

Liz and I were both avid readers, bringing many books with us as we moved in together. One day in 1995, Liz showed me a book entitled "Westland - The Journal of John Hillary - Emigrant to New Zealand, 1879". Liz's maiden name was Hillary, and John Hillary was her great-grandfather.

The book recounted the story of the Reverend J. Berry, an agent employed by the New Zealand government, who toured Britain in 1879, promoting the advantages of life in New Zealand to the public. He eventually arrived at Tow Law, a small mining town in County Durham, where John Hillary and his family lived.

John, a shopkeeper, was also a very religious man. He was a Wesleyan preacher whom Reverend Berry easily persuaded that a much better life for him, his wife, and his family was waiting in the "Promised Land." He said it would be possible to make one's fortune there.

On 27th November 1879, John and his family departed England aboard a clipper ship called "Westland." After a highly eventful voyage that would last a hundred and five days, the family disembarked at a quarantine station on Ripa Island. From there, they were taken by rail via Lyttleton Harbour to their destination—Christchurch.

What happened next turned out to be an enormous disappointment because John and his family soon discovered that New Zealand was in a state of economic depression.

Life there was not too dissimilar to the one he had left in England. In fact, it was perhaps a little worse.

So, after six months of enduring frustration, despair, and poverty, John and his family decided to return to England. This time, they came back aboard a steamship called the S.S. "Tararua," which, unlike the Westland, called at several ports on its journey back via the Suez Canal.

The long journey home must have been filled with a mix of emotions: sadness at having to return home, having failed to find the success they had hoped for in a new land, but there was no doubt some pleasure at the thought of seeing family and friends back in Tow Law.

Fortunately for us, John had decided to keep a diary during both voyages, and he also wrote a summary of his time in New Zealand. The book that Liz showed me was written by John Haddon Hillary, John Hillary's grandson, and her second cousin.

John reproduces the diary exactly as his grandfather wrote it and, where appropriate, adds helpful and explanatory comments of his own.

The book was initially published in 1979, and a second edition appeared in 1995, which is the one I read.

It was not until much later in life that I began researching my family history. I had retired, my children had grown up, and genealogical sites were becoming more available online. I completed a study of the Etches, my own family, which led to me writing some articles for family history magazines.

At the back of my mind, I had always planned to write an article about John Hillary's unfortunate venture but, as I began to map out the story, I realised that to do it justice it would almost certainly have to consist of three episodes: the outward voyage, life in New Zealand, and the homeward journey and aftermath.

I made a few attempts at this but eventually concluded that the best option would be to publish a revised edition of the book, especially as, when I re-read it, I discovered that, with the advantages of the Internet, I would not only be able to enhance some of John Haddon Hillary's comments but also to add many additional and informative ones of my own.

So, here it is....

I have retained the comments in John Hillary's diary exactly as they were previously written, apart from occasionally adding punctuation and changing spelling to clarify meaning. I have also included many of John Haddon Hillary's comments, especially those in which he writes intimately about his grandfather and relatives.

Unfortunately, he passed away in 1998, but I hope he would have been pleased with my revisions and additions. In the text, I refer to him as JHH, although I am told that his family and friends always knew him as "Haddon."

Chapter 1
EMIGRATION

During the second half of the 19th century, New Zealand ran an intensive campaign to encourage people from various parts of the world to emigrate there. Under a scheme promoted by Julius Vogel, who served as Prime Minister from 1873 to 1875 and again in 1876, the government began offering assisted passages to selected migrants and those nominated by relatives.

The message was clear: New Zealand was a fertile land, free from starvation, class conflict, and overcrowded cities. An outbreak of rural unrest in Britain had already encouraged farm labourers to undertake the long and arduous voyage to New Zealand in search of a better life.

In 1879, an agent acting on behalf of the New Zealand government, the Reverend J. Berry, came to England for that purpose. He toured Britain extolling the virtues of his home country, even creating the impression that it was a place where fortunes could be made.

His journey led him to Tow Law, a small town in County Durham, nestled on two hills approximately a thousand feet above sea level. In this area, "law" means a hill, and "tow" is the old vernacular for "two." During this period, it was a bustling coal mining town situated amidst several coal seams. Coke ovens dotted the fells, and there was a foundry within the town itself.

Living there was John Hillary, a shopkeeper who was deeply religious. Upon hearing the enticing speeches of the Reverend J. Berry, he decided that, as only the truth could emanate from such a source, he would act upon the advice and emigrate with his family to the Promised Land.

John's grandfather, Thomas Hillary, a coal miner, was born in 1781 in Marrick, Yorkshire. His wife, Mary Siddell, whom he married in 1806, was born in 1785 in the nearby hamlet of Booze, Arkengarthdale, which is situated in the Yorkshire Dales. Here, the couple set up their home, and it was here that their eight children were born.

Their second child, a son, was born in 1811 and named William. On Christmas Day, 1833, in Auckland, Durham, he married Margaret Gibbon Cree, who was born in Newcastle in 1798.

The 1841 census describes William as a coal miner living with his family at Oaks, Evenwood, just over ten miles south of Tow Law. The couple had three children: Mary Ann, born in 1834; Thomas, born in 1836; and finally, John, the main subject of this story, who was born in 1839.

In 1846, the family moved to Tow Law itself, and William became the "bank keeper" at the old Royal George Colliery. This role required him to oversee coal dispatching and to organise the workforce. Additionally, new mine shaft sinking operations had begun at the nearby Hedley Hope Colliery, and soon, William was promoted to become an inspector there.

But for many years, no doubt exacerbated by the nature of his employment, William had been suffering from asthma and heart disease, and he was soon forced to retire. He became involved in a grocery business at Dan's Castle and spent his final years running a shop. In 1858, at the age of forty-seven, he died.

His son John, who at the age of thirteen had been sent to learn a trade, returned to assist his parents in their grocery business. Following the death of his father, he carried on the business for twenty-one years. He also became a committed Wesleyan preacher.

On 17th June 1861, at the age of twenty-two, he married Elizabeth Bainbridge in Thornby, Durham. Elizabeth was born in 1841.

The Bainbridge family was among the early railway pioneers, and this was instrumental in bringing Elizabeth and John together. When the railway line through Tow Law was proposed,

Elizabeth's father, Joseph, was put in charge of operations, and he and his family took up temporary residence there. As John's father, William, was the colliery manager at the time, it was almost inevitable that the two families would meet.

John and Elizabeth had nine children in total, but three died in infancy: Margaret, Frederick, and Frederick Herbert. The six surviving children in 1879 were William, aged 17; John Tom, aged 15; Albert, aged 11; Edith, aged 5; Frederick Charles, aged 3; and baby Herbert, who was nine months old.

On Friday, 21st November 1879, having said goodbye to his mother, Margaret, John, Elizabeth, and their six children departed from Tow Law railway station on the 2:30 p.m. train to Plymouth, which was almost certainly the longest journey they had ever undertaken.

As a local preacher and social worker, John was a highly regarded figure in the town, and one can imagine that he and his family would have been given a rousing send-off. The members of his Bible Class, who met on Tuesday evenings, presented him with a Bible. The dedication read, "Presented to Mr. John Hillary by his many friends on the occasion of his leaving for New Zealand, as a very small token of their affectionate esteem."

John decided to keep a diary of his adventures, and this document forms the basis of this book.

After a "tedious ride" through "a cold and stormy night" and a four-hour stop at Darlington, the family arrived at Plymouth railway station around 11:00 a.m. the following morning. One can only imagine how the family of six children, aged six months and upwards, must have felt, having endured the most prolonged and arduous journey of their lives in an unheated train. And their spirits would not have been raised by what was to follow.

They were met by an agent of the New Zealand government and taken to a depot where they would remain for a few days until they could board their ship. Here, John said, "Our hearts almost failed us". In his diary, he states that he was confronted by almost three hundred people, mostly of Irish or Scottish origin, who were all eating in one room, with about ten at each table. He describes many of them as being "of the lowest type".

Mess tickets were being distributed, allowing the family to hurry to the kitchen below to claim their meal. This consisted of "one and a half loaves of bread with a piece of butter on a plate and a can of tea". Later, at dinner, they were served a "flat brown dish with a partition, having meat on one side and unpeeled potatoes on the other."

However, John does add that the food was "plentiful and good", and the beds were clean, but the married couples' beds were positioned in narrow stalls that were only three feet wide, and it was difficult in the night to alter one's position or to turn over. He adds that for "couples of larger proportions," it would be impossible to move.

Once the mess was over, the families had to clear the tables, scrub them down, put the forms on top of them, and wash up. There was an enclosed yard that people could walk out to or remain in one room. But John described this as being "amidst concertina playing, singing, shouting, whistling, stamping, screaming babies and all the hideous noises by which people could disturb each other, and make the place more like hell".

After breakfast the following day, John and a few others attended a service at a new Wesleyan chapel where he heard the Reverend Banham from Bristol preaching mission sermons. In the afternoon, the family took advantage of the fine weather by walking along the town's quay and streets. It was fortunate that they did so because, upon their return to the depot just before 5:00 p.m., they were told that they now had to be confined to the depot until they could board the ship.

More emigrants were arriving on every train, and the depot was becoming "crowded to suffocation." John was finding the place unbearable as by now there were four hundred people "breathing the vitiated air of one room, one hundred sleeping in one bedroom, only one stove to which poor, starving people can go, and that covered by babies' linen which mothers are trying to dry, W.C.'s filthy, no comfort."

With six young children present in his own family, the situation must have seemed like hell. John says that most emigrants "are of low class" and were not so much affected by the conditions, but he added that several respectable people had tears in their eyes as they faced such treatment.

Another worry was the threat of disease, which John commented on, saying, "If this place has not sowed the seed of disease among these two ships' passengers, it will be well." Although he may not have been aware of it then, the vast increase in emigrants had made it necessary for an extra vessel to be chartered. Had this not happened, he and his family, or at least some of them, might not have lived to see New Zealand.

This second ship was called the "Earl Granville," and later in this book, we will learn about what happened to the passengers who were unfortunate enough to have travelled aboard her.

On Monday, all emigrants had to have their luggage examined before departure. There was much confusion about what could be taken on board. Some people brought feather beds, which were not acceptable, and they either had to sell them for a small amount or simply leave them behind.

The following morning, the family was examined by a doctor in the depot's surgery, and they were relieved to find that everyone was in good health. Then, in the afternoon, it was time to load everyone's luggage onto a barge, which then carried it across to the ship, which was anchored in Plymouth Sound.

As this was the last day in the depot, the chaplain of Plymouth came along in the evening and conducted a service. His wife handed out tracts intended to "spread the Light of the Gospel," but John was not impressed, writing somewhat sarcastically that the chaplain had "considerably diluted his address and that it might be adapted to our weak capacities."

He probably realised that the chaplain and his wife were wasting their time, commenting that the "Irish made a lot of derisive noises outside," but he commended him for his attempt.

Chapter 2
THE "WESTLAND"

At last, the big day had arrived.

Immediately after dinner, everyone was ordered to gather their things together and, as families, pass briefly before the doctor once more. Contract tickets were handed out, and everyone then walked through the gate to the clipper, which was called the "Westland," and was at anchor beside the depot wall. The Hillary family must have been relieved to put the past few days behind them and look forward to the beginning of their momentous journey.

John wrote that once on board, the evening was spent pacing the deck and singing. He wrote, "We had on board 50 married couples, 55 single men, i.e. over 12 years old, 71 single women, 52 boys under 12, 44 girls, 10 infants, and 36 officers and crew, making a total of 368 souls."

The scene aboard the ship that evening must have been wonderful. Plymouth Sound is one of the most beautiful harbours in Britain, and one could imagine the joy and excitement of the passengers as they paced the deck, singing and contemplating their high hopes for the future.

The "Westland" was an iron-hulled, ship-rigged vessel built by Robert Duncan & Company of Glasgow. She was known as a "clipper ship," which meant that she was very long and narrow. Her construction was only completed in 1878, and she was of the very latest design: her hull was made of iron rather than wood, which had previously been the norm. She was roughly 223 feet long with a 35-foot beam.

This was a time when power-driven vessels were being developed in increasing numbers, but the "Westland" was such a fine ship that, given favourable conditions, it could attain speeds capable of competing with the power-driven vessels. It had been built specifically to compete, and the Hillary family must have felt themselves lucky to be travelling in such a fine vessel.

John Hillary was determined to maintain a journal of his voyage, and we are fortunate that despite the vicissitudes he and his family faced during the eighty-seven-day journey, he was very diligent and managed to record so much.

The daily entries are reproduced here exactly as they were written, with only minor grammatical and punctuation changes. The comments are made by me, as well as many from JHH.

The Westland

Thursday 27*th* November 1879

First day on board. All excitement making ready to start. Anchor weighed, during the singing by the sailors of "Goodbye, Farewell etc", and at 12 noon the fine ship "Westland" towed by the steam tug

"Secret" started her long and perilous voyage to the Antipodes. Passed by the Eddystone Lighthouse and very soon the breeze catching our ship, the tug was no longer needed. We one after the other began to feel "Oh, my," and hurried to our bunks below all drunk without drink. When I got down the hatchway I said, "Kind friends, I'm feeling very queer" and was soon into my bed. Had a rough night, and most of us were very sick. The constables came round with slop pails and another utensil which I shall no more minutely describe than by saying it resembled in shape "grand-father's hat". These utensils were soon in great demand. Cries and groans proceeded from all sides, not only from the children but from strong men and women as though caught by a terrible panic or epidemic; others lay still as pallid as death.

Friday 28th November (First day's sail of 24 hours) 296 miles

We all spent this day in bed being very sick and ill, Mamma and Edith especially so. We are now in the Bay of Biscay and are experiencing heavy weather. Many who had long neglected now lifted their voices to Him who "calms the roaring seas" for protection. The ship rolls and pitches fearfully, seas break over her and quantities of water come pouring down the hatchways. The few who can keep up are kept very busy ministering to the wants of the sufferers who are thankful for a drop of cold water. Some are very ill; their upheavals being distressing to hear. "Barney", cries a big Irishman, "she's going down". "Let her go", responds the other, "I don't care where she goes, I'm dying". "Dennis, fetch here a bucket", cries another, "for I'm vomiting my pluck". "Jim", cries the woman in the next bunk to ours, "we are going down this time, Lord have mercy on us". The hatchways are covered with tarpaulins to keep the seas out, and the effluvia between the decks on account of the sickness is becoming very unpleasant".

Saturday 29th November (Second day) 306 miles

After a terrible night about 6 am we passed out of the Bay which has been the awful destruction of so many gallant ships and the winding sheet of so many emigrants not the least the Rev D.J. Draper of the

"London". Whiting and I lifted up our hearts to God in thankfulness for His mercy. Are doing 13 knots per hour with a strong side wind and the sea is very tempestuous. The sailors say that we have already done as much as some vessels have done in 23 days and are promising to make a very quick passage. A quarter to 4 pm, sighted a French ship which being lightly laden is fearfully tossed by the furious waves. Sometimes she seems almost swallowed up and gone then she rises like a cork and is upheaved almost to the clouds. Those on deck are holding on to anything they can to seize for life. Many of our adult passengers are still very sick and many of the children. Doctor Russell has a busy time of it. Mrs. H. being helpless I have had to wash some of the baby linen this evening. Mrs. C. Neil has presented her husband with a baby while coming through Bay. It is named Westland after the ship.

John and his family are now experiencing the reality of sailing in horrendous weather conditions. However, I suspect that they were determined and strong-minded, and well-equipped mentally to face the conditions that had now beset them. We must bear in mind that the "Westland" had not been designed to be a passenger vessel, and the hold they found themselves in was designed for the stowage of cargo rather than people.

The rise of steam-powered vessels made it increasingly difficult for windjammer owners to compete with freight carriers. Instead, they had taken advantage of the lucrative trade in transporting emigrants to New Zealand and bringing wool on board for the return journey. As a result, the cargo holds had only collapsible bunks installed, with flimsy curtains that provided minimal privacy.

The hatches had to be battened down during storms to prevent seawater ingress because the decks would become completely awash. Air conditioning did not exist, and there was very little ventilation of any sort. The stench must have been appalling, and many people were seasick, especially at night when the only available light came from basic oil lamps and the sea was buffeting the hull and crashing over the decks.

It would be especially frightening for the children, and in Elizabeth Hillary's case, there were six children to care for, one of whom was only a few months old.

The Rev. D. J. Draper, whom John refers to, was a Wesleyan Methodist minister who was born in Wickham, Hampshire, in 1810. He began his career as a carpenter, but in 1830, he joined the Methodist Society and later moved to Wales, where he became a preacher.

Ordained in 1835, he had already committed himself to travelling to the Australian colonies to spread the word of Methodism. Arriving in Hobart in 1836, he spent the next thirty years working in various locations, including Parramatta, Bathurst, Sydney, Adelaide, and Melbourne.

During his tenure, he oversaw the construction of churches and schools in cities and surrounding towns. Notably, he played a key role in founding Wesley College in Melbourne in the early 1860s.

In 1865, he returned to England to represent Australia at the British Methodist Conference and to promote the achievements of Methodists in Australia. In February 1866, he and his wife boarded the steamship "London" to return to Melbourne, but tragically, six days later, the ship sank, and nearly everyone aboard perished.

Draper reportedly refused the chance of rescue and was heard to say repeatedly, "Oh God, may those that are not converted be converted now", as the ship went down. This heartbreaking event occurred just one day after Wesley College in Melbourne had been officially opened.

He would have been a heroic figure in John Hillary's eyes.

Whiting was possibly another passenger who was a Methodist.

John also mentions Doctor Russell, who was having "a busy time of it." This will not be the only time his name is mentioned in his journal.

John diligently recorded the sea mileage: 296 miles on the first day and 306 miles on the second, totalling 602 miles in 48 hours. This was excellent going under sail. Few steamers could manage this feat at the time.

Sunday 30th November (Third day) 263 miles

Beautiful morning and a fine breeze. Sighted another ship about noon. Making rapid progress all much in improved health. The wonders of "The great deep profound" this marvellous apocalypse of God shut my mouth and fill me with reverent awe. Like the psalmist I cry out "Oh God etc" Psalm 104. Feel a longing for the habitation of God's House, depressed because I cannot keep Holy Day with His people.

Monday 1st December (Fourth day) 238 miles

The roughest day we have had and people sick on all sides some seriously ill. Ship rolls fearfully. Our family is all bad except for little Fred who is the best sailor. I am obliged to move about and being so dizzy have had two nasty falls on deck. Mamma says when she writes home, she will dissuade anyone intending coming, but I suppose this is another of the speeches women make in haste to rue in their leisure. A week's rations given out in the messes.

Tuesday 2nd December (Fifth day) 158 miles

After a rough night the storm is but slightly abated. People with wry faces are sitting about on deck evidently very feeble. Passed a ship going in the same direction but not nearly so fast. Scarlet fever has already made its appearance among the children. Are bringing our beds on deck for an airing. Berths are very close and warm.

John mentions that he has had two falls on deck, and no doubt others aboard experienced the same fate. Stormy weather returned after a lull on 30th November, and he says, "Ship rolls fearfully." The "Westland" was not fitted with stabilisers, and with three enormous wooden masts, each well over a hundred feet high, and with a narrow beam, clippers were noted for rolling under certain conditions.

Wednesday 3rd December (Sixth day) 228 miles

A beautiful day and all on deck enjoying the sea breeze, much improved. Sighted the island of Tenerife which is 12,336 ft above sea level. Remained on deck until after 11 pm.

Thursday 4th December (Seventh day) 64 miles

Are this morning about the same place as we were last night, with Tenerife Peak before us and a contrary wind. Are making no progress. Am told ships are becalmed sometimes here for a week.

Friday 5th December (Eighth day) 47 miles

Are still dodging about the coast of Tenerife this morning. A small Spanish schooner passed us this afternoon and we signalled and spoke (to) her. Also sighted two other ships. All recovering. At eventide were favoured with some propitious wind and got away. At 10 pm are going about 7 knots and passing the last of the Canary Islands. John Tom while looking over the ship's side had his hat struck off his head by a rope and it was lost.

The "Westland" made only forty-seven miles, the lowest so far. This was a familiar tale, just like the hare and the tortoise, and it would be quite possible for one of the old "steam kettles" to catch them up. The reliability of steam was beginning to tell. Steamers could guarantee to deliver cargo on time; sailing ships could not, although they occasionally exceeded expectations. However, with the improvements in engine power, this slight advantage was soon lost.

Saturday 6th December (Ninth day) 105 miles

Are going well. Had a death on board and a burial. We never knew of her illness until startled by the news of her death, we skinned and threw the body overboard mourning only the loss of the mutton. While I was writing this afternoon John Tom walked up with two loaves of his own making, his Mamma laughed heartily at them. Willie is busy making a pudding for Sunday's dinner. The provisions are good in both quality and quantity, excepting the bread which on account of the heat is rather sour. Weather beautifully fine and sunny and we can hardly realise the fact that Christmas is so close upon us and yet we are apparently in mid-summer.

Sunday 7th December (Tenth day) 203 miles

Passed a brig this morning and hoisted the British flag, which was replied to, and a conversation went on for some time between the captains by means of the ensigns. In the morning Dr. Russell read the church service on deck and in the evening, I was requested to preach, which I did from "If ye being evil etc". Just as I had got to the marrow of my discourse Captain Wood came to tell me he was very sorry to interrupt but the ship was out of her course and would have to be turned. We had therefore to break up abruptly. Weather very warm especially so at night. We can scarcely bear it in bed even without covering. Having no wind, we are almost standing still at night.

Monday 8th December (Eleventh day) 39 miles

No wind and doing very little. Week's rations served out also a supply of lime juice. This tropical heat is intense being 146 degrees in the cook and bakehouse. Quite a stir on board on account of greybacks having made their appearance on the outside clothing of some Irishmen. Doctor ordered their beds to be brought on deck and searched about eight times, and had their persons stripped and scrubbed in a large tub of water and disinfectants behind a screen. A great treat was afforded us in the evening, witnessing the gorgeous beauty of an eastern sunset of which I had heard so much, but it beggars description. Often think of friends at home and wish I could entertain them an hour by recital of what I had already experienced.

We would refer to "greybacks" today as lice, and it was fortunate for the passengers that Doctor Russell appreciated the seriousness of the situation and could take the appropriate remedial action. The beds had to be searched eight times, and those affected had to be scrubbed clean and disinfected. The doctor's action probably saved many lives. Although John may have appreciated the seriousness of the situation, his diary entry was overshadowed by the beauty of the sunset.

Tuesday 9th December (Twelfth day) 50 miles

Weather lovely but rather too warm. Had a grand concert on deck tonight, the passengers and crew going through a lengthy programme in good style. Dr. Russell presided and Captain Wood led off with "The Sexton" as the first song. This was a relief to the monotony of sea life to those whose tastes were in that line, but, oh how I thought of my class at home assembled in a better cause and longed to be with them.

Wednesday 10th December (Thirteenth day) 118 miles

Weather very warm. Are now in the tropics and have had another supply of lime juice. Going about 6 knots per hour. Saw a lot of flying fish today and one alighting upon deck was an object of much interest to the passengers. They are a little larger than a herring and very pretty, fly about 50 yards at once and then return to the water. I was watchman from 4 to 7 this morning and just as I came on duty another little "Westland" was added to our number (Tarling). Am thankful he did not come to our berth for I have quite plenty to look after. Are not sorry that the Shaw Savill & Company's "Trevelyan" had not discharged her grain cargo in time, and that the Company had to charter Pat Henderson & Company's "Westland" for us, as she is such a good sailor, so roomy between decks, and the provisions are so plentiful that we cannot use them all. We have fresh bread daily and fresh water. Milk (condensed) twice and preserved meat once for the children daily. Weekly we receive loaf and moist sugar, butter, flour, suet, raisins, rice, oatmeal, pickles, carrots, onions, soup, pepper, salt, and mustard, preserved meat, salt beef and pork, also porridge (burgon) every morning. We often have to refuse taking articles as our tins are full. We can have anything we make cooked in a few minutes, and many are living better on ship than they did at home. Ship is (I am told) provisioned for eight months.

John refers to porridge as "burgon," which, as far as I can tell, is a word that doesn't exist. I think he means "burgoo," a kind of stew made from a combination of meat and vegetables.

Thursday 11th December (Fourteenth day) 147 miles

This was a busy day taking the unwanted baggage out of the hold and opening our boxes, putting away all our heavy clothing and taking light clothes out suitable for the weather. Our children were well pleased with the apples and oranges Uncle kindly put in for them, and their father was not less pleased to get his field glass and fiddle out, but especially the box of fragrant weed sent him by Messrs. Harvey & Davy, which smoked so well. The loaf of "brown Geordie" was moulded, and jam and marmalade split in the box bottom, but thanks to the liberality of the New Zealand Government we had no want. My glass was an object of much interest, and many were interested to know where I had come from, and what I had been to receive such tokens of respect. Am told by several I should do well in N.Z. but that is all to try yet.

It was a busy day indeed. The memories of the Bay of Biscay were forgotten, and as they approached the Equator, it was time to get into their "light clothes." However, one must remember that we are in the Victorian era, and T-shirts and shorts were not yet known. Men would still wear long pants, vests, and long-sleeved shirts with collars. The ladies would wear skirts with several petticoats, often reaching to the ankles, and more intimate undergarments that extended down to the knees.

The "glass" was a telescope that the members of his Bible class had bought for John as a going-away present. As a teetotaller, John would not frequent a pub, but he looked forward to his Tuesday Bible class as his weekly entertainment.

Friday 12th December (Fifteenth day) 154 miles

Nothing particular to report excepting that the heat gradually increases as we near the Equator, especially do we suffer from it at night while in bed. Many passengers are unwell on this account. Sighted a large vessel near us and got a good view of her with the glass.

Saturday 13th December (Sixteenth day) 140 miles

School commenced this morning. Several porpoises seen near our ship. Are becoming quite adapted to "a life on the ocean wave" and forming friendships. Have got our sea legs and can trot about on deck easily. Often think about how our friends at home will fear that every gale they experience will affect us, little knowing what a beautiful, mild climate we are now in, and how, when a little gale does arise the noble "Westland" laughs it to scorn and proudly rides over the angry billows of the restless sea. How dark our friends are about a sea voyage, and so were we until we got this experience. Could I sit down one evening at home I think with what breathless silence they would listen to me for two to three hours.

John is in good spirits. Wistful. Relaxed. Sailing under pleasant conditions. There was no sense of movement unless one looked through the ship's porthole.

Sunday 14th December (Seventeenth day) 79 miles

A beautiful morning. We spent a restless night on account of the heat, the thermometer registering 85 in the berths. We mustered at 10 am for the service; after calling the roll the Captain sent for me to preach as Dr. Russell felt himself unable to read the service. We had a good company, and I addressed them from "The Great Supper" – Luke 14. The Skipper seemed to enjoy it and spoke very favourably to me. Afternoon we sighted not less than 5 ships, one of them being a magnificent steamer. I took out my glass (thanks to my class) and was surrounded by people asking for a look, we had a splendid view. This eventful day closed with the death of our last accession, baby No.2, and a grand tropical thunderstorm. Talk of lightning, well, the heavens opened and the electric fluid lighted the sea up for miles and played and quivered upon the ship, awfully grand, and to say it rained is no description, for the waters above the firmament seemed to join those of the sea. The sailors enjoyed it very much.

Monday 15th December (Eighteenth day) 127 miles

The infant's remains were early this morning quietly added to the vast number who, at the last blast of the "angel's trumpet" shall arise from the mighty deep. Sugar, tea, rice, oatmeal, butter, etc. are accumulating and I cannot find room to bestow all my goods, as the cannisters are all full. After dark we sighted a fine steamer passing by us at about 8 miles distance, with my glass I could see the lights in her cabins.

Tuesday 16th December (Nineteenth day) 83 miles

Sighted 5 ships in the morning, but they were all a good distance off us. The heat is so intense I slept on deck last night. Joined my class in spirit, at the time I thought they would be assembled, but this is difficult to ascertain as the ship's time is taken from the sun and is almost two hours behind London time. Felt a great need of spiritual fellowship and private prayer, no opportunities being afforded. Making very little progress.

Tuesday was the evening when John attended his Bible class in Tow Law. So, it's not surprising that his thoughts have turned to it this evening.

Wednesday 17th December (Twentieth day) 53 miles

Sighted 3 ships, and my glass was highly spoken of by judges, but I am wearied with the number of people wanting a look every time it is out. Had one of nature's grandest panoramas in a splendid sunset, which baffles my descriptive powers, as it would also the limner's skill, its beauties we shall never forget. Another concert on deck this evening, when a lady sang "Far Away" very touchingly, and this was especially so to us under existing circumstances.

John's "glass" is turning into something of a mixed blessing!

He uses the word "limner" rather than "painter," which is perhaps more appropriate as it refers to an illuminator of manuscripts or, more generally, a painter of ornamental objects.

The song sung at the concert may well have been "Over the Hills and Far Away." It is a traditional English song dating from the War of Spanish Succession. It was used to encourage the recruitment of soldiers in England. The song was then adapted for the Napoleonic Wars for the same purpose.

Over the years, the words changed many times, and the version that John heard may have been a love song, written by Thomas D'Urfey, about a lovelorn man named Jocky who has lost his heart to a lady called Jenny.

Thursday 18th December (Twenty-first day) 92 miles

Three vessels in view when I came on deck before 6 am. It is said one of them left London about the same time as us, but as Mr. Phillips, the first mate says, when we get the wind, she'll soon be left behind, for the "Westland" can beat all competitors with a good wind. As every man's horse is the best so must sailors crack off their own ship, but I find from statistics Mr. Phillips's statement is borne out by the passages she has made. Some curious little fish swarm close to the ship's side today, about four inches in length and resembling a toy boat. They are named Argonauts, but the sailors call them Portuguese Men of War. Sometimes whole fleets of them may be seen sailing past with their purple sails up and rowing with their tentacular or feelers out, but on being approached in go the tentacular and down sinks the miniature sail as the fish concentrates itself into its shell and both vanish together like a fairy of the sea. Quite a commotion on deck today one of the single men having been robbed of two pounds his whole capital. I think a stowaway among the sailors may know something about it. Dr. Russell posted up a notice that cash or valuables could be deposited with him up to the end of the voyage. Almost all of us embraced the opportunity. Heat almost unbearable, thermometer registering 86 in the berths and 140 in the bake and cookhouse. Many are struck-out with the scarlet rash, prickly heat and suffering from diarrhoea.

It is not surprising that Mr. Phillips, the first mate, feels proud of the "Westland". The records indicate that it was an extremely fast ship, achieving an impressive number of speedy passages. On one occasion, during the wool season, despite being the last of a fleet of twenty ships to sail from New Zealand, she arrived back in England twenty-two days before the other vessels. She was even loaded and ready to set sail again before the first ship in the fleet of twenty, the "Wairoa", reached London docks.

Friday 19th December (Twenty-second day) 86 miles.

All beds and bedding on deck this morning having the parasites brushed off them, of course I refer to the Flannagans and the McFaratys many of whom are getting to be very lively. Mothers are all busy washing and we fathers are busier nursing. Oh, the joys of married life.

Saturday 20th December (Twenty-third day)

The Dr. put me on the dicky brigade this morning, the beds and bedding all brought on deck and searched. On the whole they were very clean, but we found a few alive and several dead skins on the beds of some of the Irish people. This day towards its close was a most eventful one. The sailors were on the ship a week before the passengers and as the wage for them is to receive a month's salary in advance on signing articles this was the end of it. The end of the first month is with them always a time of rejoicing for as they term it, they have been working for a dead horse and now their wages begin to accumulate. They celebrate the event by making a sham horse and stuffing him with straw, tar, pitch or any bituminous substances and placing him upon the wheel of the gun. They paint black or mask their faces put on the most ridiculous cockades, long rope whiskers, white skirts or red coats. One of them being seated astride the horse having an effigy of a wife and baby behind is drawn by the others as with lighted torches in their hands and headed by a flag they procession the deck singing as only sailors can sing and playing sackbut, flute, tin whistle, tin can and all kinds of music. On arrival at the Captain's cabin door one of them dressed the most ridiculously holding up a large wooden mallet turns auctioneer and after calling the sale by a trumpet, sells his horse to the highest bidder. A collection is then made and everything being pre-arranged horse and rider are drawn up to the yardarm when the sailor rider strikes the horse with a blow in the side with his knife striking fire, he then cuts the rope letting the burning horse drop into the sea while the rider very cleverly holds to the yardarm and is lowered down to the deck. The burning horse can be seen from a great distance. The affairs end as usual by the sailors assembling at the Captain's cabin and each being served with a glass of the best "Oh be joyful". The day's proceedings were ended by a concert under the poop over which Captain Wood presided and at which Mr. Phillips (1st mate) sang "They all get married but me". Mr. Lesly (2nd mate) sang "Rule Britannia" and several of the sailors sang good songs. Sailors have fine voices. The heat is so intense I mostly sleep on deck at nights. Some lie in the boats, but the rats are very numerous there.

JHH confesses that he had never heard of "the celebration on board" but found it "most interesting and detailed" and thought that "it could well be unique" as there was no account of any celebration when the "Westland" crossed the line a few days later nor on the homeward journey either.

My research reveals many accounts of this maritime ceremony existing before 1845. John is correct in saying that in days of sail, when sailors signed on to a voyage, they were paid a month's salary in advance, which was spent on the clothing and equipment needed for the trip, as well as grog, women and the other necessities that made up a sailor's life. Because they had to work this payment off before they were paid again, the first month of the voyage was known as "working off the dead horse". When the month was over and they began to receive their pay, it was common for the crew to perform the sort of ceremony witnessed by John.

The Dead Horse ceremony usually took place in one of the ocean regions known as "the horse latitudes": respectively, 30-35 degrees north of the equator and 30-35 degrees south of the equator. The reason was that the winds often died away in these areas, thus becalming the ships. There is a legend that I haven't researched that states that if a ship was becalmed for an extended period in one of these regions, there was a possibility of the drinking water running out, in which case any horses, and presumably any other livestock, could well be thrown overboard to preserve water for the crew. Thankfully, this did not occur aboard the "Westland".

The song "They Are All Getting Married But Me" was popularised by the American singer Alice Gleason.

Sunday 21st December (Twenty-fourth day) 41 miles

Mustered for roll-call and service at 10.00 am. Prayers read by Dr. Russell. A nice dish of stew of my making for dinner and a fruit cake of Mamma's making for tea. In the evening, we spent some time sitting on the forecastle watching a passing ship and enjoying the cooling sea breeze. Was pained to hear the lookout man who is an old sailor of superior education stuffing some green Irishmen with big fish stories of what he had seen and done during his seafaring life. The dear boys with eyes and mouths wide open were taking all in as truth and seeing this he did pile it on. Old Joe is a notorious liar for, as a messmate of ours from Leeds observed, he is quite ahead of "Tom Pepper", and he was two degrees beyond the Devil.

According to nautical tradition, Tom Pepper appears to be a character in folklore who was banished from Hell for being a greater liar than the Devil himself.

grandchildren eat at a separate table and in another room from their parents. He would then produce his fiddle, the one mentioned in the diary, and play tunes on it, such as nursery rhymes, which would appeal to the children. JHH also states that Christmas dinner was not John's favourite meal, as he preferred his "giblet pie supper," which he would eat after the children were safely tucked up in bed.

Friday 26th December (Twenty-ninth day) 64 miles

Crossed the Equator during the night and were at noon today 12 miles east of it. Several large porpoises near the ship. They resemble a boat sailing bottom uppermost, and their broad backs rise and fall with the regularity of a ship.

Saturday, 27th December (Thirtieth day) 129 miles

Having got fairly into the South Atlantic we have caught the southeast trade winds and are going along in splendid style. The sea runs high and tosses the ship very much. Mrs H having gone down downstairs to make a cake for tomorrow's tea had a recurrence of sickness. Several are sick again today. Spoke to a ship named "Mary Stuart" from Swansea to Bolivia in South America.

Sunday, 28th December (Thirty-first day) 214 miles

This morning sighted two vessels and passed very near the island Fernando Noronha, a penal settlement owned by Brazil, it is 7 miles long by 2½ miles wide. With my glass I could see the houses, roads, fields and trees, and in an aperture between the rocks a landscape resembling some of the Weardale scenes; was to me one of the greatest treats, for after a month's view of the sea and sky only, the sight of green fields was good for sore eyes. After muster Captain asked me to take the service which I declined, because when prayers are read by the Dr, all seem to attend as a duty but when we few dissenters hold a preaching service people don't feel under any obligation to come and the under-officials go on dealing out water, bread, meat and doing whatever they can to interrupt what they consider to be a put-off service. I am anxious to do what good I can and after the kindness of Dr, and Captain sorry to refuse but it is possible to make yourself too cheap, to cast pearls before swine and by an injudicious use of religion to bring it into contempt. Read a few psalms which greatly refreshed my soul but the depth of the longing I felt for the Sanctuary of God my pen could ne'er express.

It may seem strange that the "Westland" was not hugging the coasts of Spain and West Africa as she journeyed south, but, having crossed the Atlantic Ocean, she was relatively close to the coast of Brazil. Although this decision added considerable mileage to the journey before the ship turned east towards New Zealand, there was good reason for it, and this was to catch the Easterlies and Roaring Forties – winds that blew fairly constantly along the 40th Parallel and along which the journey was to proceed for several thousand miles, passing the Cape of Good Hope.

In those days, there was no Panama Canal, and the Suez Canal, which had been open for about ten years, was useless to sailing ships.

Monday 29th December (Thirty-second day) 197 miles

Are 44 miles from the coast of South America. A busy day giving out weekly supplies. This is the first time in my life when I could live and keep out of debt without money yet have stores coming in weekly plenty to eat and no bills to meet. Had a view of the coast of Brazil, could see the trees by the aid of my glass and six coasting ships. In the evening while lying on the forecastle one of these coasting smacks passed us at speaking distance on our port side and we exchanged a shout of recognition.

Tuesday 30th December (Thirty-third day) 136 miles

Having little wind, the heat is terrible. Our day dress is approaching the primeval, our night-dress being almost quite so. The nights bring little relief on account of the air being so hot in these parts. Mrs. H. says my friends will little think that on Xmas week I am trotting about the deck with nothing on but straw hat, shirt and trousers, minus both stockings and boots. Three ships passed this afternoon and one a steamer at night. Thermometer stood at 86 in the berths at 11 p.m. Captain put a man on look-out this morning with as many eyes in his face as there are days in the year. I suppose he will keep us off the rocks. During the night had another accession to our numbers, a "gal", this must be put a stop to, we cannot have passengers or rather stow-aways coming on in this way without either paying their way or being nominated.

Wednesday 31st December (Thirty-fourth day) 145 miles

About 7.am. the "Market Castle" of Boston, a three masted schooner passed so close to us that we could clearly see the people on her deck with the naked eye. Fearfully hot, great preparation being made for New Years Day. Mrs. H. is just busy making toffee, gingerbread cakes etc. Could our friends but see the set-out at the cookhouse, their ideas of poor fare on an emigrant ship would be corrected. Thought much about the rapid flight of time, the Watch Night service which would have been my thirty-third in the old chapel and lastly how, if at home, I should have been friend M.G. Barrows' "Lucky Bird", and with a few friends comfortably seated round his festive table telling stories and trying to increase the joy of his guests. Had I been there this year, however, my recitals would have had an unusual interest for them.

Thursday 1st January 1880 (Thirty-fifth day) 219 miles

A New Year has come to all, young and old, poor and rich, the cottage and the hall. Usual congratulations exchanged on deck this morning, and as we are leaving Britain for one reason and this year will be an epoch in the life of each, we hoped it might be one of the brightest and best. Going at a rapid pace, we are many of us poorly today and unfit to eat anything. The day closed with a concert of secular songs. This is a godless place, and there is such an attempt to blend light and darkness, as well try to mix fire and water. Captain Wood asks me to preach on the Sabbath, and himself reads the lessons, yet during the week he sings songs, leads off the dance, allows much profane swearing among the crew, and himself sets the example. Gather not my soul with sinners, nor my life with bloody men.

Concerned that the reader might gain an incorrect impression of John Hillary from his comments above, JHH was anxious to describe the sort of man he knew his grandfather to be. He wrote:

"He was by no means a sour, thin-faced individual pacing the deck with a telescope under one arm and a bible under the other, preaching hellfire. He was a short man of very cheery disposition, always ready for a joke and with a ready smile. In later life, he always wore a smoking cap, but it is doubtful if this was the case at the time of the voyage. He was by now a teetotaller, though he had not by any means always been so, but he was a pipe smoker and this he remained for the rest of his life.

To understand the position clearly, it is necessary to appreciate the conditions then pertaining. John Hillary lived in an age of religious revival; churches and chapels were full, and hellfire was preached and believed in. The population was divided between the religious and the irreligious, and in the former, there was a tremendous puritanical streak that ran through the Victorians generally. As any reader of the literature of the times will be aware, they were reputedly great people for falling on their knees and thanking God for any blessing which they imagined they had received. One only has to read such books as "John Halifax Gentleman", "Tom Brown's Schooldays" and that classic of priggishness "Pilgrim's Progress" to gain some idea of the atmosphere surrounding the upbringing of many people at that time. It may be that the Victorians embraced religion because they feared going to Hell, but they were very fervent in their beliefs and decidedly intolerant of others who did not share their views. John Hillary was no different from thousands of people of his generation, and despite his sanctimonious views, was at heart a good and kindly man, ever ready to give help where needed.

It is perhaps difficult for the younger reader to comprehend fully the conditions as they were all those years ago. Life consisted mainly of working for long hours under shocking conditions, which would not be tolerated today. For most people, there were only two ways of alleviating their sufferings: drink or religion. Drink was undoubtedly a terrible scourge and the cause of much distress and poverty, and was therefore much feared and preached against. Although the Scriptures said, "strong drink is raging", it also said, "be fruitful and multiply"; thus, if drink was out, sex was in. Large families were the result, with any number from 15 to 20 children being quite normal, which did not help the situation. The Hillarys, with only six children, were relatively modest and showed an understanding not general in their day. They were to have another child, Ethel, but she did not arrive until their return to England and does not figure in the diary."

Friday 2nd January (Thirty-sixth day) 219 miles

Nothing very remarkable excepting the heat which is excessive. Although over the line by 1271 miles yet on account of it being winter at home and mid-summer in the antipodes, we are just about now directly under the sun's rays at noonday and almost melting away.

Saturday 3rd January (Thirty-seventh day) 206 miles

Lost the most unfaithful companion I ever had, for he only stood by me in the sunshine, and in the dark and cloudy day was never to be seen. However, although my shadow is gone because I am directly under the sun, I suppose I shall have a new one from the other side in a few days. We expect tonight to be out of the Tropic of Capricorn.

Sunday 4th January (Thirty-eighth day) 189 miles

Calling the muster roll, and reading a dry service by doctor and Captain, giving out dinner, water, bread, milk etc, and this holy day made for man the brightest of the seven, which was always to me such a delight at home, gives one no pleasure, but pain to see it so spent. Shut out from the services of the Sanctuary I envy those "Happy birds that sing and fly around Thy altars, Oh Most High." When the voyage is ended my greatest joy will be to appear before God in Zion.

Monday 5th January (Thirty-ninth day) 198 miles

Heat abating. Are going splendidly. Allowance of lime juice and extra water discontinued. Edith has taken measles.

Tuesday 6th January (Fortieth day) 221 miles

Another trial, Edith and Albert both down in the measles and by doctor's orders we are to go with them into the Hospital on deck. As there are other cases on board it is feared we shall on arrival be ordered into quarantine, which must be unless the passengers have been free from all infection for one lunar month. We are going with a good wind, and the hope of the officials that we shall yet make a quick voyage, seems to be reviving. We expect to reach the latitude of the Cape of Good Hope tomorrow. Thought much of my class, and a little after 4 o'clock I joined them in spirit, it being 7.30 with them.

Although both children are suffering from measles, John was no doubt pleased that the family could be transferred to a cabin on the deck, which, in effect, was like being upgraded to first class from the communal quarters below deck. The doctor has taken a great interest in the family and continues to do so throughout the rest of the voyage.

Wednesday 7th January (Forty-first day) 215 miles

Fred took measles in the night, but they are all favourably held, and we hope with good nursing may soon recover. Willie and John Tom are, of course, in the single men's apartments out of the way. We prefer the hospital on the main deck to the berths. Saw several porpoises, and a ship passed us at noon. Mamma was delighted because, with the glass, she could see people on the poop. About 3 pm, the "Famenoth", a fine ship of Shaw Savill & Company, bound from Auckland passed close by us, there was much waving of handkerchiefs and shouting on each side. It is quite remarkable; we had both been out 41 days and met halfway. We wondered to see so many passengers returning on this ship, if N.Z. is so prosperous, and England so dull, why return?

The "Famenoth" was a sailing ship, and it was highly unusual to see one returning in this direction, as it was the standard practice for them to continue eastwards from New Zealand across the South Pacific, around Cape Horn into the South Atlantic, and then reach home. Three years would pass before Shaw Savill & Company ventured into steam, and these vessels could return more easily via the Suez Canal.

John, and indeed others, wondered why so many passengers were returning on the ship and asked why this would be the case if New Zealand were so prosperous. Were the seeds of doubt being sown in his mind at this moment?

Thursday 8th January (Forty-second day) 65 miles

Children going on all right, and we are very comfortable in the Hospital, as well off as cabin passengers, having the room to ourselves. Dr. Russell visits us about four times daily, and supplies us with chicken soup, arrowroot, sago and anything the children can eat, also a bottle of stout daily for mother, so that her vigils may not weary her out. We are rounding the Cape, and the weather is very enjoyable, having left the long-remembered heat of the tropics behind. Several albatrosses flying around us, and passed through a shoal of sturgeons, the shouting and laughing at their antics in the water being deafening.

JHH comments on mother's daily bottle of stout:

"...if John Hillary was teetotal, Mamma was obviously not. As stated previously, the diarist had not always been a non-drinker, and the writer can remember his Grandmother telling him how this came about. It would appear that in their early married life, it was necessary for John Hillary to visit many of the local farms on business. While there it was customary for a bottle to be opened and a drink or two consumed, thus John Hillary sometimes used to arrive home, if not drunk at least decidedly "merry". This caused Mrs. H. considerable anxiety, which was noted by her husband, who having insisted upon an explanation, was informed of the reason. His answer was simply to stop drinking from that moment and henceforth he became a rabid T.T. It is possible that it was from then that he turned to religion, because it is hardly likely at that time that a religious person would touch drink, the two just did not mix. Certainly, if the church might condone some drinking, Chapel certainly did not, and as we know John Hillary was a non-conformist."

Friday 9th January (Forty-third day) 113 miles

Seven albatrosses surrounded us this morning, and after dinner, with the aid of a baited hook, one was caught. It is a pretty bird about 20 lbs in weight, its wings stretched out measuring from tip to tip 9 feet 4 ins. Children improving but another case has broken out on the ship. Seven weeks today *we left home.*

Saturday 10th January (Forty-fourth day) 82 miles

Have heard much about the solemnity of a burial at sea but today have witnessed one. The little daughter of J. Smith of North Allerton, aged two years, died of measles at 5 am and at 11.30 am her body was committed to the deep, until, at the fiat of Him who is the Resurrection and the Life, the greedy sea shall yield her dead. A vessel bound from London to Adelaide named "Pakwan" passed us (this) afternoon and our first mate went over to her in a boat, with letters to send home from the Cape. This caused a great stir.

I cannot find any record of this vessel, but "Pakwan" is the Tagalog word for watermelon. Tagalog is an Austronesian language spoken as a first language by the ethnic Tagalog people, who comprise a quarter of the Philippines' population, and as a second language by the majority.

Sunday 11th January (Forty-fifth day) 71 miles

The Sabbath is to me the most wearisome day of the week, inasmuch as it forcibly reminds one of those blessed Christian privileges, I enjoyed at home but am now deprived of. Reading "Service", giving out beef, water, milk and bread, and the day with a painful retrospect is gone. Children are doing well.

Monday 12th January (Forty-sixth day) 104 miles

Weekly rations served out. Some fresh cases of sickness among the children, but ours are convalescent. Dr. Russell is most assiduous and tender in his attention to them. He has tried to lance a large sea lump on Fred's head which has discharged a quantity of matter. Most people on board have these or other eruptions caused by the heat of the tropics.

Tuesday 13th January (Forty-seventh day) 100 miles

Was out at 5.30 am and saw a whale blowing up. Large flocks of albatrosses, mollyhawks (sic), Capehens (sic), Cape pigeons, and Mother Carey's chickens flying around us. Had a good wind all day and tonight the sea is running high, and the "Westland" is dashing along at a great pace.

The correct word is "mollymawk" and refers to a group of medium-sized albatrosses restricted to the Southern hemisphere. Cape hens and pigeons are called the "Cape petrel".

The term "Mother Carey's chickens" is applied by sailors to a bird known to ornithologists as storm petrels. Sailors associate them with storms and bad weather, often seeing them as a bad omen. Some believed that they were the souls of sailors lost at sea.

A mollymawk

They are tiny creatures, not much larger than a lark, and the very smallest web-footed bird known. They have a sooty-black colour, with a bit of white on their wings and tail, and because their diet consists of fish and whale blubber, it is said "they are very unpleasant to approach".

The name "Mother Carey" is thought to be an English corruption of "Mater Cara" (Dear Mother)—the appellation bestowed by Italians on the Virgin Mother, who has been regarded as the special patroness of mariners from time immemorial.

Wednesday 14th January (Forty-eighth day) 208 miles

A cool day and high sea. Glass standing at 59 in berths. Saw a lot of mule porpoises in front of the ship which swam about a mile with us. They are pretty fish with brown backs and white bellies, about 28 lbs in weight and shaped like a mackerel. They who go down to the sea in ships behold the works of the Lord and His wonders in the deep.

Thursday 15th January (Forty-ninth day) 187 miles

Several albatrosses and mollyhawks about us. Sailors busy tidying all up for making the ship respectable before she reaches Lyttleton Harbour and fastening down spare spars and boats as though there were indications of a storm and a shaking. They say we will not have any more calms and may run 350 miles a day yet, as this is a place for wind.

Friday 16th January (Fiftieth day) 207 miles

Eight weeks today we left home, would that we have another home. We do not forget pay Friday and talk of what people will be doing in Tow Law. Mamma says many of them in business will be mourning over short payments, increasing balances, pressing liabilities etc., and trying hard, like a dog after his tail, to make ends meet.

John was a shopkeeper who ran his business in what was primarily a mining community. A miner's pay depended heavily on the amount of coal he produced, and if the seam he was working on contained more stone than coal, he would receive "short pay" at the end of the week. The shopkeeper would be pressured to help the miner until conditions improved, and he would, but it made business very difficult and significantly affected profits. Could this have contributed to John's desire to emigrate?

Saturday 17th January (Fifty-first day) 191 miles

Cold weather. Herbert poorly and apparently beginning with measles. Flour and raisins given out for Sunday's dumplings. Have now sailed over 7,000 miles and are still rounding the Cape of Good Hope but going wide of it. Sailors are lashing everything moveable on deck and we think this ominous of squalls.

Sunday 18th January (Fifty-second day) 221 miles

Very high sea. Ship rolling very much. Had this been the first week we should have all been ill today. At noon our time was on a par with Greenwich. Roll called, but no service because of the rough weather. I had a severe attack of spasms about 2 am and Mamma had to send the watchman aft to the doctor, who sent me a strong dose of mint. Am better today, but sore. Water bottles, flour tubs etc. have all to be lashed and tin plates, dishes etc. are chasing each other about the floor. She pitches fearfully.

Monday 19th January (Fifty-third day) 245 miles

Water and milk at 6.30 am. Children's meat and soup at seven. To cook house to toast bread and get coffee and porridge for breakfast at eight. Sweeping and scouring under berths at 9 am. Going to store for weekly supply of sugar, coffee, tea, butter, salt, pepper and mustard during forenoon. Pea soup, boiled salt beef and carrot for dinner. Bread and butter or tinned meat and rice to tea (sic) at 5. Had great difficulty in getting our food as the ship is rolling so much, several fell on deck and our plates and food frequently fly off the form during meals. Friends at home would be terrified, but we old sailors seem to think nothing of it as we sit with the door open with the ship going down on one side almost beneath the surging waves, then rising right up above them until we have to hold on to anything we can catch to keep on deck. Time, 25 minutes before London.

The experienced sailors know what to expect regarding the weather as they lash down all movable objects. Note also how the daily runs are increasing substantially.

Tuesday 20th January (Fifty-fourth day) 203 miles

After a night of rocking on account of a stern wind we have got the wind on the quarter today, and are going smartly but steadily, a side wind is always best. Herbert continues very poorly indeed.

Wednesday 21st January (Fifty-fifth day) 252 miles

Weather cool and bracing. Having no fires to warm us we have to pace the deck to keep up natural heat. Going fast. Our baby, Herbert, is very ill and in addition to the measles has got inflammation of the chest.

Sickness is bad at home, but how much worse at sea, without a friend to sympathise with you, or a fire to warm you.

Thursday 22nd January (Fifty-sixth day) 267 miles

Eight weeks today since we set sail. Another stowaway appeared this morning, I suppose he is a big Irish boy (McGrath). Herbert is a trifle better but still in great danger. With a fog and a south wind, the weather is cold and comfortless, but landsmen hardly know what those terms mean here, for nothing wet at sea seems to dry, but retains a clammy dampness which is most unpleasant to feel.

Friday 23rd January (Fifty-seventh day) 165 miles

Baby about as yesterday. Storm expected. Caught by a line and hook a fine albatross, measuring 10 ft, from tip to tip of wings, and 5 ft. from bill to tail. Nine weeks today we left our dear friends and home. Oh, the charm of that word "home", I never felt its sweetness or valued its comfort until now.

Suddenly, the weather has turned cold. The ship is just below the latitude of Cape Town, and, although quite far away from the South Pole, it must be remembered that Antarctica is an enormous land mass that produces huge icebergs as well as a chill sea. As the wind was southerly, it must have made conditions aboard the unheated "Westland" very miserable. John and his family also had to contend with storms, the continual dampness and, most of all, baby Herbert's sickness. It is no surprise that John's thoughts are turning back to the home he has left.

Saturday 24th January (Fifty-eighth day) 207 miles

The expected storm came this morning and raged all day furiously. Mrs. H and children all kept their beds, and I only ventured out when obliged. Several people got bad falls on deck, among who was Isaac Whiting, whose feet shot out like greased lightning, and he landed in the scooper (scupper?) under the spars with such force the sailors sarcastically asked if was trying to knock the bulwarks out. A sea caught several of the single women and almost drowned them, they had to go to bed until their clothes were dried. Many got bad bruises from being dashed down, and Mr. Phillips, the first mate, was sorely hurt. The carpenter's bench was smashed, and our Willie fell and spilt his porridge. Tedious as the voyage has become to us, we should prefer being longer on the ship than having a recurrence of this day's tossing. Baby is very little better.

Sunday 25th January (Fifty-ninth day) 276 miles

The storm abated somewhat about noon, but in the morning, it was very dangerous moving about deck. No roll calls on account of the stormy weather. The thoughts of home comforts made me very sick of sea life, oh, that this voyage was ended, and its godless associations. We have much wickedness, but no prayers, no Christian fellowship, no Sanctuary. The faces, voices, forms, times and unction of the old chapel no longer to cheer me, and the people, houses, fields, and roads recur to my memory now, with a vividness no pen can describe. However, my confidence in the wisdom and goodness of that Providence who has guided me my life long and directed my way here, is as firm as ever it was. I suppose when we land, and I am employed, my mind will rest again.

Monday 26th January (Sixtieth day) 273 miles

Have still a strong wind and dashing along swiftly. Captain says he thinks at this rate we shall land in eighteen days. The weather is very cold, and having no fires to sit aside, we feel it keenly. Herbert is no better.

Tuesday 27th January (Sixty-first day) 232 miles

The first mate is able to resume his duties again after his fall. Baby is still in great danger, not having strength to expectorate the phlegm caused by the inflammation in his lungs. A sea voyage may be beneficial if short, but this one is too long and the climatic changes are exceedingly trying to adults, but too severe by far for little children.

Wednesday 28th January (Sixty-second day) 225 miles

Scores of birds flying around the ship. Weather very cold and dull. Baby worse. I must here correct a mistaken notion we had, and our friends will still have, that the sea looks flat, and you can see as far as the eye will carry. Every way you look the sea appears round, the ship always seems to be in a hollow and you think, looking ahead, you have only a hill to go over, and you will get faster away, but this is always the same. The ocean meets the sky, and the masts of a coming ship look small sticks rising out of the sea.

Thursday 29th January (Sixty-third day) 291 miles

Weather cloudy and foggy. Caught another albatross 9 ft. 9 inches from tip to tip of wings. Have been sailing 9 weeks and done 10,036 miles. Our little son is no better, and the congestion of the lungs having been so severe his recovery is very doubtful.

Friday 30th January (Sixty-fourth day) 100 miles

Dr. Russell has given Herbert up this morning, and though this news is distressing it is not unexpected, for I saw a few days ago "that death had marked him out an offering for the tomb". When friends at home read this, they will know what my feelings are today, far away on the pathless sea, friendless and homeless. Oh, Lord, give me Abraham's faith and obedience. Caught another albatross this evening 10 feet from tip to tip of wings. Witnessed this evening the most gorgeous sunset we have yet seen, but to describe its grandeur I am quite unable.

John is undoubtedly going through a very traumatic period. Not only does he face the severe illness and probable death of baby

Herbert, but he also feels the complete isolation and the loneliness of being at sea for an extended period with a total lack of communication with the outside world. He had no knowledge or awareness of what was happening there. It is difficult for us today to fully understand the utter loneliness and boredom of being at sea for weeks or months. Such travellers fully understood the meaning of "the lonely sea and sky".

Saturday 31st January (Sixty-fifth day) 57 miles

A fine day but little wind. A whale and many porpoises seen and a Mollyhawk caught. Herbert is wasting for want of support and cannot take it.

Sunday 1st February (Sixty-sixth day) 167 miles

Captain said to us at roll call this morning "Three weeks this morning you will be going to church in New Zealand". Won't that be a joy if true? At muster Captain read out some charges against one of the young men passengers named Thomas Robinson of being drunk and with some sailors breaking into the ship's stores and stealing therefrom spirits etc. They are to be prosecuted on arrival in port. Baby Herbert is still sinking.

Monday 2nd February (Sixty-seventh day) 226 miles

Have been sitting up all night with our dear baby as the presages of death are upon him. He still lingers however, but how soon we have to give him to the sharks we know not. I feel this affliction most keenly and have weakened myself by grief. "He who has most of heart has most of sorrow".

Strangely, there is still no mention of John's wife. As a mother, she must be distraught at the prospect of her tiny baby Herbert dying, but we only hear about John's grief.

Tuesday 3rd February (Sixty-eighth day) 198 miles

Herbert is a little easier, but we fear whether the improvement will be permanent. More birds caught and some of the passengers are busy skinning them, the breasts for muffs, bones for burnishing leather and pipe stems, and the skin of the feet for tobacco pouches. John Payne's eldest girl is very ill, I fear fatally so.

Albatrosses are extremely large seabirds with long, narrow wings, and they are found mainly in the Southern Ocean. They are renowned for their majestic flight and long oceanic journeys. Now that the "Westland" has journeyed into this area, it is not surprising that the number of these birds sighted by John and other passengers has increased.

What is surprising, though, is the fact that large numbers are being captured and killed. In maritime folklore, killing an albatross was believed to bring bad luck to sailors, as the birds were seen as protectors of them and their ships. Their appearance was often interpreted as a sign of good luck or the presence of lost sailors' souls. So, harming or killing these birds was seen as a grave offence that could bring misfortune upon the perpetrators and their companions.

Samuel Taylor Coleridge popularised this view in his famous poem, "The Rime of the Ancient Mariner," published in 1798. In it, a mariner shoots an albatross, bringing a curse upon the ship and its crew.

The word "muff" is seldom heard these days, but women wore them to keep their hands warm in cold weather.

Wednesday 4th February (Sixty-ninth day) 178 miles

Strange to say Herbert is a little brighter and beginning to take a little support. Weather very cold but having a good wind our ship is dashing at a rare speed.

Thursday 5th February (Seventieth day) 272 miles

Baby still improving. It is ten weeks since we set sail and to all appearances within a fortnight we shall be in harbour and thence to quarantine which seems now to be a certainty for us. However, we shall be on land and have a change of diet which will be of great benefit. We need some vegetable food for our blood is heated and skin itching.

Friday 6th February (Seventy-first day) 256 miles

A rough sea and stormy day, but we are going at fine speed. Baby much better, and to all appearances he is to escape the sharks and see the godly land.

Saturday 7th February (Seventy-second day) 258 miles

Dr. Russell says there is a marked improvement in Herbert, who is beginning to eat well. The kindness and attentions of Dr. Russell are beyond all praise, and with chicken broth, medicine, and wine would have cost us pounds in England. Another birth during the night, a "gal" (Robinson).

Sunday 8th February (Seventy-third day) 255 miles

Fine day, Sailing well. Herbert progressing. Our time now is eight hours before London, so that when our friends at home were getting breakfast, we were having tea. This we hope will be the last Sunday but one we have on board. At Dr's request I preached between decks tonight to an attentive audience. Took the parable of the "Ten Virgins", had good liberty and a blessed unction, Lord help me to live a useful and powerful life. Heard of one rather queer woman on board, making her children say prayers before going to bed after the service.

What fantastic news of baby Herbert's progress! He lived to be seventy-one years of age and, at the age of twenty-four, became the father of John Haddon Hillary. He died in Queen Elizabeth's Hospital, Birmingham, of bronchopneumonia – the same complaint that he suffered from as a baby all those years ago aboard the "Westland".

Monday 9th February (Seventy-fourth day) 275 miles

Going well. Herbert rapidly recovering. Weekly supplies of provisions given out, and no bills to pay nor any losses to mourn. Have plenty to eat, and more than we can use of some things, but the fare becomes so monotonous that the stomach almost refuses it.

Tuesday 10th February (Seventy-fifth day) 267 miles

We expect, if we keep this wind for another week, to land. Are now going along the Australian coast, but too far off to see it.

Wednesday 11th February (Seventy-sixth day) 156 miles

Wind eased about 1.am and we are now going slowly. The cold has passed away, and we are having fine weather, as we near the land of the Southern Cross.

Thursday 12th February (Seventy-seventh day) 151 miles

A second child of Mr. Tarling's died about 9 am, of dropsy after measles, and at 11 o'clock this morning we committed his body to the gaping waves. Eleven weeks today we set sail, and in another week, we hope to cast anchor in Lyttleton harbour. Sailors are busy as the "Devil in a whirlwind" making all look spliff. Herbert is almost well again; his recovery having been wonderfully rapid.

The measles virus had been the scourge of human life for thousands of years as it was very easily transmitted from person to person when an infected person coughs or sneezes. In those days there was no vaccine.

Friday 13th February (Seventy-eighth day) 215 miles

Twelve weeks today we left home. Excepting being far away and on the sea, we know nothing to trouble us, our income is nothing, but our outlay and our losses are no more, we have none of those bad pays which used to destroy our peace of mind and unfit us for life's duties. And the "begaring (sic) travellers" don't come here.

Today was baby Herbert's first birthday, but strangely John makes no reference to it.

Saturday 14th February (Seventy-ninth day) 159 miles

Postman did not bring us any Valentines this morning. Am far away from Hedley Hill today. Three Albatrosses and five mollyhawks caught today. Are on the coast of Tasmania but not able to see it. What strange Saturday nights these are, indeed as there is nothing to make any difference in this monotonous life all days are wearily alike.

Sunday 15th February (Eightieth day) 258 miles

Going well with a good wind. Payne's eldest girl is sinking. I preached this evening from the last text I used at Tow Law "Wherewithal shall a young man cleanse his way". People listened attentively and I hope good was done. Am now going to my little narrow bed, it is just gone eleven and our friends at home will only have finished dinner it being 1.pm with them.

Monday 16th February (Eighty-first day) 293 miles

Are all busy scrubbing and washing our bunks out for landing. I have been down between decks washing ours out, although it has been standing vacant during the six weeks, we have occupied the snug little cabin on the main deck.

Tuesday 17th February (Eighty-second day) 258 miles

Sighted a vessel ahead this morning and not having seen one for five weeks it caused some excitement. No ships return to England this way but keep still going on East and go round the other side of the globe, this would seem strange to landsmen. At about 6.30 in the morning our time my class will be meeting at 7.30 in the evening at Tow Law, our time being now 11 hours before theirs. What a pleasure it would be to meet them now.

Wednesday 18th February (Eighty-third day) 173 miles

John Payne having been keeping vigils over his two children all night, who are dangerously ill, called me up before 5.am, to see those black rocks or coral islands called "The Snares" in longitude 166, which we are passing. They look like the walls of an old castle in height and length. At 4.pm, we sighted the end of South Island or Otago coast round which we will go to Lyttleton. Have anchors ready to cast and expect soon to be in harbour. Tonight, the light from Port Chalmers shines brightly.

John's spirits are lifting at the sighting of the South Island. Yet, because the "Westland" was approaching it from the "wrong side," to reach Lyttleton harbour, they would have to turn south and sail around the coast of Otago, through Foveaux Strait, and then continue north until they were halfway up the South Island before arriving at their final destination.

JHH comments, "Nearly eight weeks have elapsed since any mention of land being sighted, and five weeks without even seeing a ship. In fact, although this was the 18th of February, they had not seen land since the previous year, on the 29th of December. It seems incredible these days that this could happen under these conditions. The "Westland" was far removed from the luxury line of today and, by comparison, very small indeed. There were no facilities for any form of amusement, and, with the exception of the few concerts on deck, no entertainment of any sort. No wonder the passengers were happy to catch a few seabirds and skin them, and what pastimes the children had are not mentioned. We can imagine with what longing John Hillary looked forward to the end of the voyage and, being an active man, getting into harness again. He was not to know that many months would pass before he would be at work again, and that would be in Old England".

Thursday 19th February (Eighty-fourth day) 202 miles

We are only 150 miles from port but the wind having ceased are almost standing. Had raisin dumpling and sauce, preserved meat, carrots and bread for dinner and Dr. gave half a bottle of porter and a quarter of sherry to each family. The day is beautifully sunny and warm, whales blowing up near us and numerous birds off the coast flying around us. Tonight, a rat came in at the cabin door and terrified Edith and Fred until we got it caught and killed.

Friday 20th February (Eighty-fifth day) 100 miles

Are almost becalmed on the coast such are the uncertainties of sailing ships. A fair wind would easily have put us in the harbour this afternoon. Sails are altered every few minutes and we are sailing backwards and forwards but are not able to round Banks Peninsula, from whence a revolving light shines brightly tonight. Seaweed in great quantities and land birds attract our attention, also a small red fish, like shrimps in size, called sea spiders, in such quantities as to make the water in some places appear as red as blood.

Saturday 21st February (Eighty-sixth day) 50 miles

After drifting about several hours near the shore this morning with a foul wind we hailed a pretty steamer bound from Timaru to Lyttleton by which we asked to be reported. The Captain treated us kindly and promised to report us and the cook stepped to the door of the galley and smilingly held up a leg of mutton before our longing eyes. Afternoon a steam tug named after the harbour came and towed us in. By the mercy of God, we are anchored in the splendid harbour of Lyttleton. We had not been anchored many minutes before a boat came alongside us and put an abundance of provisions on board, the flesh including a whole carcass, the vegetables, bread, milk and eggs, etc. being all fresh and good. That we regarded them as dainties I need hardly say. My diary will now show my varied experiences and feelings during the voyage, but all my hopes of the beauties of the place and the fineness of the climate are fully realized, and the discomforts of the voyage seem already to be disappearing. But that we are ordered into quarantine is another trial, however, we hope it won't be long before we have our liberty again.

Sunday 22nd February

We were this morning taken off the "Westland "and landed at the Quarantine Station on Ripa Island which is almost opposite Lyttleton about 3 miles across the bay, and 3 acres in extent. The buildings, which are neat and clean, are all wooden, painted and covered with corrugated iron. We can fish, bathe and enjoy ourselves.

So, finally, after eighty-seven days at sea, John Hillary and his family disembarked from the "Westland", a ship that had been their home for almost three months. Later in this book, we will learn more about what became of John Hillary and his family. But, what about the "Westland"? What became of her?

I have already mentioned that she was built in 1878 by Robert Duncan and Co. in Port Glasgow. The owner was Albion Shipping, which was registered in Glasgow. In 1882, the company merged with Shaw, Savill & Co.. Around 1906, the ship was sold to C. Hannevig of Norway. Not long afterwards, having left Barbados, she ran into such bad weather that she had to be put into Kingston, Jamaica, where she was condemned and broken up. It was a sad end to such a fine ship.

One name stands out like a shining light throughout John Hillary's daily entries: Doctor Russell. When Baby Herbert was ill, we read about the four visits he paid per day, and it is fair to conclude that without such attention, Herbert would not have survived.

We also read about the wine and soup, which John admits "would cost pounds in England," and the doctor's "many kindnesses." Although he seemed to have a special affection for the Hillary family, there is no reason to suspect that he only showed his kindness to them.

I mentioned earlier that two ships had to be commissioned due to the large number of emigrants. In this next entry, as John resumes his journal after his quarantine on Ripa Island, we learn about the fate of many passengers who travelled aboard the "Earl Granville."

Friday 12th March 1880

Were taken off Ripa Island by the little steamer and via Lyttleton, by train, arrived at Christchurch in the evening. We lodged the first night at Mother Bleigh's restaurant where we found a good cup of tea and the soft beds very acceptable. Next morning we set up house in New Street, where we had to pay 12/- per week in advance for a four roomed wooden house with (a) cooking range so useless that we could not cook our food, and after remaining here three weeks we removed to King Street, Sandridge, into a better house at the same rental. Here we remained until the six months of our colonial life were ended, and we returned home to England. In finishing the diary of our outward voyage let me again refer to the den of disease, the Government Depot at Plymouth, where the seed of the fatal disease on the two ships was doubtless sown. The bad arrangements and crowded state of that wretched place arose from the fact that the officials admit some of the filthiest specimens of the human race, whose dirty persons must engender disease, and in our case the emigrants for both the "Westland" and the "Earl Granville" were brought there at the same time and crowded together like a flock of sheep. Besides the sickness and deaths on our ship, the New Zealand newspapers reported that when the "Earl Granville", which left Plymouth two days after us, arrived, about 100 passengers had died, beside the doctor, the remainder were in quarantine, and they were dying like rotten sheep, and filthy with vermin.

The barque "Earl Granville" was a fine iron vessel of about 900 tons. It was commanded by Captain Campbell, under charter to the Shaw, Savill & Co.. She arrived at Auckland on 4th March 1880, having sailed from Plymouth with 318 Government immigrants aboard.

Ten days after leaving the Channel, measles and whooping cough broke out among the children. In all, there were about fifty cases, but only three children died. When the vessel reached port, there were six cases of low fever, Dr Fox being one of the victims.

Dr Philson, the health officer, ordered the vessel into quarantine, and she proceeded to Motuihi, where all the passengers landed.

However, for Dr Russell's constant attention and vigilance, such could have been the case aboard the "Westland" when lice first appeared. There were deaths, but they were proportionate for the times and did not result from Dr Russell's lack of attention.

Lyttleton Town and Harbour

Chapter 3
THE PROMISED LAND

I don't know if, during John's stay in New Zealand, he maintained his daily journal; considering the conditions he and his family found themselves in, that is not surprising. Perhaps he made brief notes and waited until his return home to Tow Law before writing up his experiences. But, at some point, he put pen to paper and produced what follows in this chapter. Apart from minor grammatical and punctuation errors, I have made no changes. The following words are exactly as John wrote them.

"CHRISTCHURCH: A city of 24,000 people standing on the sides of the serpentine river Avon which is crossed by 20 bridges and on the banks of which the stately Poplar and Weeping Willow grow so luxuriantly as often to meet at the top and form an arch over the river. Like the new Jerusalem the city lieth foursquare, its streets, which are 50 to 70 yards wide, run parallel from east to west and north to south crossing each other at right angles and are a mile in length from belt to belt of the city proper. This however only represents about one third of its extent. The streets have grown so far over the town belt, and it is intended soon to extend the belt to two miles, but even when the streets grow to five miles the same order will be maintained.

The houses which, excepting for business places in the centre of the city, many of which are brick or concrete, are nearly all built of wood and stand detached upon quarter, half or acre sections of land. They are very pretty many having a good deal of taste displayed in their design, are nicely painted with verandas in front on which stand a couple of chairs, and a grass plot or flower garden in front. Some of them have fountains playing all year round, for perhaps Christchurch is the best watered city in the world. It is often said it stands upon a latent reservoir, and it is a remarkable fact that you have only to tap the rock and the water gushes out.

Suppose you build a house, you select a place in your garden for your well, then employ a professional artesian well sinker. He puts a pipe plugged at one end with about one inch bore upon the spot, puts a rod up the inside and a heavy weight with a hole up the middle to fit the rod upon the pipe. He then fixes up three legs and a pulley which he puts ropes across and pulls the weight up and drops it upon the pipe until it is driven to the proper stratum when he drives out the plug and the pure water flows up with great force. A bend-pipe is put on the end and a box placed beneath; the outflow being turned through the garden into the street so that in the heat of the summer the pedestrian has a cooling stream of water flowing by his feet. The water is left running and never dries up. Two or three days before washing the wife takes her dirty linen in a coarse bag and lays it into the box, where it steeps and bleaches as white as snow.

THE PEOPLE: The Maories are tall, robust and not treacherous like most aboriginal tribes. The Europeans are clever, sharp, shrewd, respectful but very selfish people. He who goes out expecting to teach them anything will be mistaken. Even children, well-educated and quick. Sharp but pretty talkers, accent Yankee and Cockney.

RELIGION: In a declining state. The people seem so engrossed by this world their energies are all used up. Although they have fine churches and contribute freely to the cause, they do not care for much experimental preaching.

COLONIAL PHRASES
Shout for all round.

Chuck.	Clear out.
Go for him.	Vault.
Good on you.	Up a tree.
Cooie.	He done to me.
Gassy. (too much gas)	Staunch horse.
	A terror.

Get the smell of lime juice and pea soup off you.

OPINION OF NEW ZEALAND: Climate, all that it was represented and quite equal to our expectations. More equable than that of England and so much finer that winter is as good as an indifferent English summer. The sky is so clear and the atmosphere so thin that the sun, moon and stars seem to shine far brighter, and the distance is so difficult to estimate that mountains and objects 50 miles away don't appear to be over 5, and photographs taken here are far clearer than those taken at home.

Many garden flowers remain in bloom all the year round and the trees don't cast their faded leaves as at home. On the shortest day of the year, we have daylight from 7 am to 5 pm. Twilight short. Even in mid-winter the days are generally sunny, sometimes very warm so that a man cannot work or walk freely with his coat on, but at sundown he must put an extra one on. For although the nights are not as cold as English winter nights, the heat of the day thins the blood so much that the nights are in Colonial phraseology a "Terror for cold".

The heat of the summer is very little more than at home but even then, so cool are the nights, sleepers can always bear the blankets upon them. The extremes between day and night are far greater than in England.

Walking along the foot of the hills and by the side of the Heathcote river on July 18th, corresponding to January in England I sat down on the river's bank and almost wept out loud because I could not make my way in such a fine country, and to all appearances would be obliged to leave it.

The river as clear as crystal is fed by artesian springs bubbling up in its bed and springs flowing out of the hillsides pouring into it. The gorse (whins) was covered with its yellow flowers, which is in bloom all year round and the sides of the rivers were studded with majestic poplars. The drooping willow and the flax plants reminding me forcibly of those pictures in our Missionary presents of those Eastern Countries "where every prospect pleases and only man is vile". Soil – some of it very rich but a great quantity almost worthless. The great drawback to the land is that beneath are beds of shingle of several feet in depth.

A farmer took me into one of his paddocks (fields are called paddocks in N.Z.) and beneath a soil of 16 inches there was a clean shingle bed of 9 feet, and he told me in a dry season this land was as bare as the back of his hand. Otherwise, the soil is light and clean and rarely a stone to be seen. With a wheeled plough the farmer can read a book or a newspaper on the stilts of his plough all day long. Vegetables grow to a large size and potato disease is unknown, but the land produce sells for very little at present.

WORK & WAGES Having read Agent General's Hand Book and Rev. J. Berry's Pamphlet, I expected statements therein made as to abundance of work, high wages etc and general prosperity of New Zealand to be true. What was our surprise on landing to find hundreds walking the streets who could not get a day's work. Prospect being so dark we saw the necessity of moving very cautiously and having taken a four roomed house at 12/- per week in advance, purchased £6.10, worth of furniture and a cwt of coal for 3/-, we started housekeeping, although in poor heart.

Albert got work at a boot factory at 1/- per day. Willie called upon the builders and only one gave him any hope. This putting-off disposition found everywhere prevailing, was simply disgusting after the straightforwardness we had been used to at home. "Get the smell of lime juice and pea soup off you and then call again".

Willie's first engagement was three days as a pantryman at a restaurant called "His Lordship's Larder", next about three weeks serving a stone breaking machine and afterwards 3 months ploughing with Mr Boon, a farmer at Riccarton, 6 miles from Christchurch, for which he was paid 10/- per week and tucker.

John Tom was first employed hawking scones and pastry for a baker on commission but could make nothing at it. Afterwards he got a fortnight's work at the stone-breaking machine, and then at Mr. King's soap works at 15/- per week.

Having gone round the City and been unsuccessful, I called upon the Rev. Mr. Reid and presented my credentials. I called upon the employers whose addresses he gave me, they took my address and promised if they had or heard of anything they would inform me. Called again and again, offered to work hard at a boy's wages at anything, but never could get an engagement. During the six months we were there I was in turn cobbler, painter and carpenter but only for a casual day, and only earned 12/- in the country.

I know of nothing that knocks the man out of you and makes you feel so despicable in your own sight as when looking at wife and children and being powerless to help them. I felt thoroughly miserable and determined to do anything that was honest. Went out one day with my tools soliciting lamps to repair and earned 3d. Went out two days seeking houses to paint, leaving addressed envelopes with the people, also advertised for painting but got nothing.

As a soup kitchen was being opened called on the Mayor of Christchurch explaining my position and asking if a man would be required there. He enquired what my wife was doing and if she could not go out or take in work to help us. I replied that after cooking, washing, mending and housekeeping for a family of 8 she could not be expected to do more, to which he replied, "Oh, I have known women with larger families make a lot of money sewing, etc." I could not say to him what I felt at such ungallantry, but my manly spirit stirred within me and, as I turned away the thought that in the prime of life I should have, when willing to do anything I could, to depend on the earnings of my wife, caused the tears to gush from my eyes.

The soup kitchen is open daily by a committee with the Mayor at its head, who also distribute coal, clothing etc. to the suffering. Meetings of hundreds of unemployed are held in the Cathedral Square almost daily, who are signing petitions to the United States and Canadian Governments asking them to send a ship for the hundreds who are bordering on starvation.

Much indignation is freely expressed, several of the most conscientious tradesmen joining, and the newspapers publishing letters and leaders charging home upon the Government the inconsistency of inveigling people away from their comfortable English home by means of exaggerated and one-sided lectures and pamphlets, to sorrow, untold suffering, disappointment and despair.

A clerk, a new chum, not being able to get work took to book hawking and the day he called upon us he said from that day week he had not taken a penny. Another clerk called about the same time who having been out 15 months and got nothing, was trying to sell vinegar at a small commission.

Another, Mr. W. Raine, had only had a few hours carrying the monkey for the masons and returned with Mr. Williams on the S.S. "Cotopax".

A very respectable man named Hawkes, an ironworker from Sunderland, having after paying passage for self and family out and being in Christchurch for months and never having a day's work resolved, rather than stop and be totally ruined, also to return. He had just sufficient to pay ocean fare and intended asking the rail company at London to keep their luggage as security and send them on free home until they could raise the money and redeem their luggage.

Met a family of father, mother and two sons who paid their passage and came out from Bradford shortly after us. They were printers by trade and had been in one of the best establishments in England at a good salary, had read the pamphlets and were persuaded. It was pitiful to hear their regrets. Could not get a day's work and took to hawking tea but found this a played-out game and next door to begging.

The older son, who was a widower, with much emotion and tears, told me they would never settle and be happy until they were home again, and if friends in Bradford only knew their position, they would subscribe to pay their passage back. Mother was out at work and at harvest time the three men would go up country harvesting, work hard and save every penny until they could raise passage money.

On July 3rd I had a conversation with Mr. Wallas, a bootmaker in the Colombo Rd. who came out 6 years ago and, although the eldest son had made his way, his large family scattered, some up country at farm stations whom he seldom heard of, and he finished by saying he would rather have England with one meal than all New Zealand had to offer.

Mr. Mets, a shopkeeper in Colombo Rd. who is a general dealer showed me his takings, and on the first 3 days of July he only took 2/11d and seldom more than 35/- per week while his rent and gas amounted to 34/- per week without rates, thus leaving him with only 1/- to buy goods and keep his family. He said it was no good crying.

I met a man in Christchurch who came out to Wellington also from Bradford, a short while before us, where he gave up a good tinsmith's business. He brought a patent machine for making tins and £700 in cash. When I met him, he had lost all his money and been at Weka Pass where, although he had a family left at Bradford, he was paid 21/- per week and had nothing left to send home.

A Mr. Sykes told me of a man from Hull whom he knew, a carpenter by trade, who could earn 50/- per week at home. He came out here and is now at Weka Pass at 21/- per week. Their bread having run out he and another went to a "Station" but, instead of receiving the "proverbial hospitality" the Rev. J. Berry speaks of, they were neither given any food nor allowed to go near a fire and turned into a hen roost for the night.

On September 1st I called at five places asking for employment, and Mr. Taylor, ironmonger, of Cashel St. told me he was from Canada. Several friends, for years, pressed him to advise them to come out to New Zealand, but he would never advise one of them, even in New Zealand's best days. When he was on a visit to Canada a few years ago a gentleman met him and asked for his advice. Mr. T. told him if he could float at home, he was to give up all thought of New Zealand.

He was a gentleman worth some £10,000, and strange to say, he sold out, spent all his capital chartering a little ship, loading her with agricultural implements which, with his family, he brought out. When he arrived in New Zealand the farmers would not look at his implements and scouted the idea that if they were adapted to Canada, they would be suitable for New Zealand. Mr. T. says the last he heard of him, he was sitting on the rocks on the seashore crying like a child, without a shilling left, ruined.

The Agent General's "Hand Book" and the Rev. Berry's pamphlet, when they state the wages in New Zealand should also in all truthfulness state that men do well who work three days per week and that most men are only half timers, and many work hard for a time and never receive any wages. The following facts which were given me prove this.

A shipmate of ours, a mason named Davies, finished his first contract at building chimneys and his boss filed his petition and swindled him out of his earnings.

I met a man this afternoon, Sept. 3rd who came out on the "Orari" thirteen months ago. All the work he had was 3 months with a threshing machine for which he was to receive £1 per week and tucker.

Unlike home, thy don't profess to pay a man until the job is finished, and when he went to seek his wages, his boss was "up a tree" and he never got a penny.

When the gallery was put into Colombo Rd. church, where we attended, two carpenters took the contract for the whole and sublet the plasterers and painters' work. The painters were of course the last to finish and, on the day following the two carpenters drew the whole £600 and filed their petition swindling the plasterers and painters out of every penny.

Mr. Wilson, curer and leather merchant also told me that during the last three years he had lost £3,000 and £1,000 during the last nine months by bankrupts who never paid 1d in the pound.

Mr. Butcher, a London man, a bricklayer, told me his house was in his wife's name and when I asked the reason, he said he was obliged to have it thus so that when people for whom he worked "filed", merchants could not come upon him for material.

Mr. Millar, who has 8 houses in King St., the street we lived in, was building the ninth when we left. All his property is in his wife's name and every bit of wood he gets she must stand for. He has gone through the courts so many times that when he made his last appearance the Judge told him that the next time, he appeared there he would inflict the highest penalty in his power for fraudulent bankruptcy.

To show what those lecturers who came over to advocate New Zealand care for the people whom they induce to go out, Mr. Gibson, a gentleman from Scotland who came from Dunedin on the "John Elder" told me of a minister named Isis who was over in England and Scotland advocating New Zealand some time ago.

Two men, one of whom was a manager of a Co-Op store in Manchester, followed Isis out. Mr. G. says that the last time he saw that man he was going about the streets of Dunedin with a bag picking up pieces of potato and coal to make a fire and roast the potatoes to keep body and soul together.

The other man, starving, found the Rev. Isis and asked him what he could do for him; he turned his back and cooly said "Nothing". Sorry to have to speak thus of Ministers, but what respect can we have left for men who will so disgrace the sacred office as to stoop for money to such disreputable work.

Of the passengers who went out with us very few had any work when we left. Mr. Howard from Consett had only had about 12 days' work in an office.

Mr. Richards only got a casual day's work now and again. His wife had been confined, and he had been idle for three weeks and reduced to the last shilling, but a shipmate had given him 2/-. When in our house, his blood boiled when speaking of the Rev. J. Berry who, by a letter, had advised him out, as he also did me.

Mr. G. Rogers, a carpenter, from London, having had very little work, had been obliged to sell a brooch and earrings value £3 which were presented to Mrs. R., who was a Wesleyan teacher trained at Westminster and had recently been an accountant in a warehouse in London.

A Mr. Spencer who told me he was willing and able to do a day's work with a pick and shovel against any man but could not get a living in the country. He had been up the country at 8/- per week and with loss of time through wet weather, difficulty in getting material for want of roads etc. after paying for his tucker, he brought home to wife and large family £4 for six weeks, which after paying 8/- per week for two rooms and 2/6 per cwt for coal, left them 2/10 per week to keep the lot. He added that he could do far better at home with 3/6 per week and wished me to publish his statement. He also said the Agent General on this side seemed very particular about character, but in New Zealand his testimonials were never looked at, and the biggest scoundrel was in as good a turn as the most respectable man.

Mr. Phillips left a situation at 50/- per week and never got any work in New Zealand. When we left, he was swagging up country and wrote his wife saying he had forded three rivers in one of which he was nearly drowned, he was still wandering and had got nothing. I never saw such an object of distress as Mrs. P. was. Her eyes were sunk into her head, she had pawned her wedding ring to buy the little girl a pair of boots and expected butcher and baker to stop supplies daily.

She said if all Christchurch were her own, she would give it to get back to Old England again.

Cashell Street, Christchurch looking west across Colombo Road

JHH writes, "There is no doubt that John Hillary was very unlucky and arrived in New Zealand at the time of the worst depression that country had ever known. The gold rush had subsided, and the price of wool, which was the country's chief and almost only export, had fallen heavily on world markets. Being an up-and-coming country, many goods were required from outside, and while imports were rising, exports were falling rapidly, creating a balance of payments problem. Thus, money was leaving the country, and little money was returning to replace it.

Had John Hillary been a man who had mixed in financial circles, there is little doubt he would have been made aware of the true position and not undertaken such a journey at that time. On the other hand, being only a tradesman in a small and not very prosperous community, he felt he could improve his position in a new country.

We must at least admire his courage and determination to succeed. In later years, members of his family were to criticise him for returning so quickly and not staying and facing the position.

It can be argued that it was, in fact, unfortunate he was able to find the money to pay for the whole family to return. Had he not been able to do this, he would have been forced to stay and see the thing through, but under the circumstances as he found them, to have chosen to remain would have required great courage, and it was a hard decision to make."

JHH did not know how John Hillary found the money to pay for the passage home, but he assumed that he had most likely left money behind in safekeeping with his brother, Thomas, in Bishop Auckland, and he sent the necessary funds.

However, many of the immigrants who arrived had no option but to persevere, and it would be interesting to see how they eventually fared. I'm sure they will have descendants living quite happily and prosperously in New Zealand today.

Within ten years of John Hillary's abortive attempt to settle, though, an invention was produced that would put New Zealand back on its feet again. It was the invention of the refrigerated ship, the first of which, the "Dunedin," sailed from Port Chalmers in February 1882, that enabled New Zealand to export its frozen mutton and dairy products, thus giving the country a new prosperity that continues to this day.

Chapter 4
HOMEWARD BOUND

After spending six months trying to find employment and with all hopes of a happier future in the "Promised Land" firmly dashed, John Hillary and his family decided to return to England and were undoubtedly delighted to start on their homeward journey. John must have become thoroughly disillusioned and extremely bitter towards the Rev. J. Berry, who had persuaded him to emigrate to New Zealand.

However, they could not sail directly to England: they had to board a small coastal steamer bound for Australia and, from there, catch the larger vessel that would take them back home.

Unlike the family's outward journey aboard the "Westland," which was full of joy and anticipation of the success and happiness that would await them, this return voyage must have been tinged with feelings of sadness and frustration. In John Hillary's case, there must have also been some excitement at the thought of returning to his beloved "class," as each day's voyage came and went, he was a little closer to it.

Tuesday 7*th* September 1880

Left Christchurch by the 2.40 pm train and Lyttleton at 4 pm on board the Union Company's S.S. "Tararua", a dirty but strong and seaworthy coasting ship. We were all rather sick, especially the children.

The "Tararua" was built by Gourley Bros. of Dundee in 1864. Classed as an Iron Screw Steamer she was approximately the same length as the "Westland" but of somewhat narrower beam. She did not rely solely on the engine because she had three masts on which sails were hoisted when the wind conditions were favourable. Roughly six months after the above date, on 28th April 1881, she was wrecked in extremely tragic circumstances on Waipapapa Reef, New Zealand, with the loss of 102 lives, including women and children.

The wreck of the S.S. Tararua

Wednesday 8th September

Arrived at Port Chalmers at 1.30 p.m. and remained overnight in the harbour.

Thursday 9th September

Left Port Chalmers at 3 p.m. having taken on board a lot of passengers who are returning home quite disgusted with the state of things existing in Otago.

Friday 10th September

At 7.am. we landed at the Bluff, the port for Invercargill. Here a Danish woman in Mamma's cabin presented her husband with two little stowaways. The Bluff is a miserable looking place, the moorland round it much resembling Hedley Hill banks. We left there about 2. pm., passed through Foveaux Strait where we had a good view of the lower end of Otago and Stewart Island and, soon getting into lumpy water, our passengers, one after the other, soon felt that they had dined off German yeast and began to cast up their accounts, and such a night we passed for storm, rolling and pitching as I hope never again to experience. The strong old "Tararua" laboured so heavily, and the seas struck her with such force that she shook from stem to stern, and we feared we would be dashed to pieces.

Hedley Hill was a small mining village in County Durham, between Tow Law and Esh Winning. The expression "casting up one's accounts" meant to vomit, and the reference to German yeast possibly meant beer.

Saturday 11th September

Very few can appear at breakfast table this morning and these holding on by both hands to their bunks and looking amazed as though they were just coming out of a terrible nightmare. A very stormy day and a tempestuous sea. So far, our passage has been a very rough one even for the coast of New Zealand with its reputation for storms and where so many lives have been lost.

Sunday 12th September

Rather better weather and a few got on deck, but they were poorly. J.W. (John Willy) says if he had not booked through, he would have had no more of it but stopped at Melbourne, so tired is he of the voyage already, it makes him so ill. The wind having shifted from the head to the port side, we have got some sail on, and the old boat does not roll so much. What joy it is to be journeying home to old England, the land of Christian privileges and Christian Sabbaths. I could wish the weeks without Sabbaths such as they are, for they only give me pain, but a few more and I shall regain them in their sweetness in my dear old house.

Monday 13th September

Had beef and potatoes to breakfast. A very wet uncomfortable morning. Going about 10 knots per hour. Old Jack Taranacki, a passenger is very ill and calling for some canvas to stitch him up in. No wonder, for yesterday he only consumed 2 bottles of lemonade and a tin of sardines, all the oil of which he drank because the steward told him it would make him strong. He is very ill and groaning like a dying horse. A gale springing up at noon, the sea is again running dangerously high.

Tuesday 14th September

Had a terrible night and all were much alarmed. Heavy seas were shipped and in one of them tons of water must have been heaved on deck by the furious elements for the shock nearly sent us all out of our bunks and the old steamer trembled under it for some time. All are lightheaded this morning. A passenger (is) missing, a tall gentlemanly looking man. He kept in his bunk all yesterday suffering from neuralgia, and we think that either the rheumatism has struck his desperate brain and made him a suicide or having occasion to go on deck during the stormy night, when sailors could only with difficulty keep their feet, a sea struck him overboard. As he is not now on board then the only sad alternative is he is added to the myriads who are buried beneath the wild, wild waves. From a pocketbook found in his overcoat it appears his name is Michael Carr, he has been sixteen years farming at Leeston, near Christchurch where he has left his wife and children. Having cleared out, he was on his way to Victoria to buy land and make a home. The storm has abated. Passed Tasmania in the evening.

Although it is now fair to describe John as a seasoned traveller, the weather he is experiencing is much worse than that he endured in the Bay of Biscay, and he is expressing more concern. Perhaps he feels that, as people are falling overboard, his current vessel is undoubtedly not as safe as the "Westland".

Wednesday 15th September

A fine morning and a calm sea, a double quantity of edibles consumed at breakfast table. At 10.am we are on the coast of Gippsland, which is ninety miles from the Heads, and 130 from Melbourne. At 5.pm we have a fine view of the Australian coast from opposite Shag Point. It is not so rugged as the coast of New Zealand. At 7.pm we entered the harbour and were tugged up the Yarra to the wharf which we reached at midnight, glad to step on terra firma once more.

Thursday 16th September

Took lodging at the London and Carnarvon Hotel at 17/- per day, best we could do. Uncle Richardson came to see us in the evening.

The charge for the whole family would be 17 shillings, not individually.

There are no entries for the 17th or 19th September, probably because John and his family were visiting relatives. I can find no information about Uncle Richardson.

Saturday 18th September

Went at Uncle's expense to Newlyn, John James meeting us at Daylesford station with their buggy and a drive of 11 miles brought us to their pleasantly situated and hospitable home, where John and Robert Richardson came to see us and enquire after the welfare of all Tow Law friends.

Monday 20th September

Returned to Melbourne, James drove us through the diggings 7 miles to Creswick, a pretty village where Robert Richardson came 4 miles in his buggy to see us off and brought us a large fine home-fed ham for use on the ship. Stopped 3 hours at Ballarat, a good sized, well-built and clean town and about half an hour at Geelong where

C.T. Richardson met us. Geelong is also a town of considerable size, but of course in all these places the activity and the excitement is a thing of the past. After travelling by this route 170 miles, we reached Melbourne at 4.pm. Victoria is very much like the north of England but not comparable to New Zealand for beauty.

Tuesday 21st September

Went on board the "John Elder" the fine steamship of the Pacific Steam Navigation Company at 9.am and at 12 noon started upon our return voyage to old England. Passengers were besides Britons, Germans, Italian, Swedes, Frenchmen, 1 Norwegian and 1 Arab. The Frenchmen who had been exiled after the Franco-Prussian war to New Caledonia for 10 years and their term having expired, were returning to Paris.

The "John Elder" was built by John Elder & Co. of Glasgow and completed in August 1870. On 18th January 1892, during a voyage from Valparaiso to Liverpool laden with copper bars, ingots, ore, silver ore, and general cargo, the vessel ran ashore at Carranza Point, about sixty-five miles north of Talcahuano and became a total loss. Her crew and passengers were saved, however.

The John Elder

Wednesday 22nd September

Strong head wind and rough sea. It was very dangerous venturing on deck during the day, but the night was a terror for storm. The sheep, pigs and cattle suffered severely, indeed some of the bullocks had their lives almost knocked out of them. A seaman had his shoulder dislocated and a passenger some ribs broken, and one boat was smashed.

JHH writes: "The Hillary family were certainly having their share of stormy weather, and there was more to come towards the end of the voyage. It is unlikely that stabilisers would be fitted to the "John Elder", so the sufferings of the passengers must have been quite severe, the more so as we have reason to believe our travellers would be in what was then known as "steerage". This, as the word implies, was in the extreme stern of the ship, just over the screw and rudder, where most of the motion and noise would be experienced. At least the passengers had the advantage of knowing what it was all about, but what of the poor, dumb animals that had to be carried to provide fresh meat? Their suffering must have been appalling. A small but interesting point is the use of the expression "A terror for the storm", a colloquialism then in use in New Zealand and, after six months, already acquired by the diarist".

Thursday 23rd September

Tempest still raging and a strong adverse wind hinders progress. Four bullocks in a dying state were killed for their hides and their bruised and blackened carcasses thrown to the sharks.

Friday 24th September

Early this morning arrived in Adelaide harbour and cast anchor glad to find shelter from the stormy weather of the Australian coast and the perils of the great deep.

Saturday 25th September

A busy day taking in passengers, cargo and coal. Sad accounts by passengers of the state of the colonies. One young man from Nottingham has only been out six months, earned but £5 swagging and lying in canvas tents and is a loser by £90. A family from Staffordshire named Davis have been eight months in Wellington and they will be £400 out before they get home. A mason from Haswell has been two years in Sydney and Melbourne doing sinking and anything else and is obliged to return because he cannot live. A young man from Belper who left home two days before us has been swagging in New Zealand is also returning. He tells me he has spent £350, and a very respectable man named Terrell, a wheelwright, who has lived near Adelaide for 20 years is returning with wife and children to London, disgusted with the discomforts and uncertainties of colonial life. This evening a boat came alongside bringing us 8 bullocks; they were a savage lot and had killed one man in capture. Seven of them were hoisted on deck by steam winch and a rope round their horns, but the 8th slipped out and swam ashore again. All busy making ready for a start.

"Swagging" means carrying one's personal belongings in a bundle.

Sunday 26th September

Early this morning we set sail again and soon got into lumpy water with a strong head wind. Ship heaves very much. We have had a rough passage so far. Lord of the Sabbath bring us safely home.

Monday 27th September

Sea somewhat settled during the night and today we are going along smartly yet pleasantly at 12 miles an hour. Had a conversation on deck with a man who came out from Preston in Lancashire eleven months ago and left a situation of £2 per week upstanding. He returns with a deficit of £90 and is thankful he left his wife and two children at home.

He had 5 months' work for which he got wages and afterwards 3 months of heavy wet work, but when he went to draw his wages, his boss was "Up a tree" and he got nothing.

The expression "Up a tree" can have two meanings. One is being drunk, and the other, which is the more likely one in this context, is to be in a challenging or troublesome situation. So, perhaps the boss had gone bust.

Tuesday 28th September

A strong side wind is propelling the "John Elder" swiftly along, but a nasty sea is running. Killed the lean calf and two sheep and cast another bullock overboard.

Wednesday 29th September

Wind light but fair, clear sky, weather warm and pleasant. Oh for "Home sweet home" and some employment, a life of idleness is to me a life of misery.

Thursday 30th September

A great change of weather, strong wind and heavy sea. Ship labours heavily and staggers under the heavy seas which strike her. I was greatly distressed during the night, having dreamed that Jonathan Hodgson had been killed by a fall of stone in the pit. I sympathised with his family.

Who was Jonathan Hodgson? JHH comments that he believed that the event described above by John did take place, but adds that, as far as he knew, Jonathan Hodgson was not a relative but was possibly known to him in the small Tow Law community and was perhaps a member of his Tuesday Bible class.

With the benefit of the Internet and a genealogical site, I began to search for Jonathan Hodgson, and, to my utter astonishment, I discovered that on 28th January 1884, a miner with this name was killed in an accident at the Black Prince colliery, Tow Law. Details of the accident state that he was "severely crushed by a fall of stone in a broken jud".

In mining technology, a "jud" is the depth of coal in the face that will fall after being undercut.

The 1881 Census says that he was born in Etherley, in County Durham in 1831, eight years earlier than John, and his wife, Isabella, was born in Ridsdale in 1850 – so she was quite a bit younger than her husband. The couple had three children at the time of the Census: Margaret, aged 10; Jane, aged 8; and Isabella, aged 2 – all of whom were born in Tow Law.

JHH hints at the possibility of John's dream being a sign of paranormal premonition by saying "...such phenomena are still being investigated today, without as yet any feasible explanation".

When John returned home in 1880, Jonathan was still alive and working in the Black Prince mine. I wonder if John ever saw him again, and, if so, did he mention his dream to him?

Friday 1st October

"Rocked in the cradle of the deep". I am sick of the sea and wished we had been rolling up the Thames this morning. Day got out fine but cold. Killed a bullock, sheep and a pig. Have passed Cape Luin.

Saturday 2nd October

Fine sailing weather. I blacked all the children's boots and my own. Doing 300 mile a day.

On his return journey John no longer provides his daily mileage. Probably he feels no need to as, unlike the "Westland", the steamship could maintain the same speed every day, which was a consistent 300 miles.

Sunday 3rd October

A Sunday but no Sabbath. Oh, for one Tow Law Sabbath. What a Godless place this is. The regulations say this Holy Day is to be kept as religiously as circumstances will permit. I see no change either in work or wickedness. Morning Captain read prayers in the first saloon and evening a cursing steward officiated in the steerage, but I did not attend and countenance such blasphemy, for how can blessing and cursing proceeding out of the same lips glorify God. Fine breeze. Warmer weather. Pleasant day.

Monday 4th October

A warm morning and very little wind, yet such is the advantage of steam as well as sails we are going rapidly. The "John Elder" is a fine built steamer, 150 yards long, fitted with hurricane decks. Draws 25 ft under water and has three decks above it. Has 24 fire holes and 27 firemen and consumes 50 tons of coal per day. Carries 450 souls, including officers and crew, £156,000 in specie, thousands of bales of wool and 2,000 tons of coal, besides other valuables making her cargo one of the most precious ever brought from Australia.

Tuesday 5th October

A fine day and propitious wind. How on these Tuesday evenings I long for the sweet fellowship of God's people in class assembled.

Wednesday 6th October

Weather becoming hot. Killed a bullock a sheep and a pig. Albert has gone to assist the saloon cook, his remuneration being better "tucker" for self, Father and Mother. This is very acceptable, the rations of the third class being uneatable. A lot of us waited upon the Captain and Chief Steward this morning taking a sample of the greasy rice served up for our breakfast and requesting that in future the boiled rice may be sweetened with sugar instead of being boiled with fat meat.

The Captain promised our request should be granted. As very little was eaten, that remaining was given to the pigs, but they pitched it out of their troughs and with a grunt turned up snouts. A passenger at sea should have stomach like a sausage machine, able to digest anything.

On the outward journey, John and his family cooked their own food, which, as emigrants, they had no reservations about. However, on this return journey, they were fare-paying passengers and must have expected something better than the swill that was served to them, so inedible that the pigs turned their snouts up when it was offered to them.

Thursday 7th October

After a hot night and little sleep have cast off drawers, stockings and flannel shirt. Saw about 100 flying fish in one shoal this morning, they are only to be seen in warm latitudes.

Friday 8th October

Excessively hot and the nights bring but little relief. Sailing about 300 miles daily. The Arab passenger, Ab Dallah, who has been ill since leaving Adelaide, died at noon and at 1.pm a respectable looking Irishman took a fit on deck and is very ill from Excessive heat. Yet who cares for sickness and death on board ship so long as they themselves are well, no one sheds a tear or heaves a sigh. "Has he any money?" I overheard a passenger smilingly ask the Frenchman who acted as attendant and interpreter to the Arab as he came out of the hospital when the last offices were performed, and the spirit had fled. "Here is the coffin" cries the sailmaker with a laugh as he jaunts along the deck with the canvas on his shoulder. "Have you got the cold meat stitched up yet", asks a steward in derision, as though he himself was immortal. As the law requires that corpses at sea be buried within 2 hours, at 2.pm this poor disciple of Mahomet was without a sigh or a tear or a funeral note, the engines merely stopping for a minute and the sailors raising their caps, committed to the great grave of the Indian Ocean.

Which I am told is 11,000 miles long, 10,000 broad and averaging 4 miles in depth.

A Welshman named Broad, in the next cabin to ours has been in New Zealand and New South Wales for 5 years and never had a chair to sit upon. He says he sometimes returned home from work so exhausted by hard toil and heat that he could not unfasten his shoes, until health and strength failed, and the doctor told him if he worked 6 weeks or more, he would be in his grave. At 28 years he looks 40 and returns home, I fear, to die. He tells me he knows two men who went out to New Zealand, one being a schoolmaster at home with 12 children and the other a postman with 10 children. He says he never saw men so disappointed. Not being able to get work they bought canvas tents and went into the bush where all working, they could hardly get salt. The schoolmaster sometimes did painting when he could get it, or anything else, but they were almost reduced to starvation.

The expression "he never had a chair to sit upon" is often used metaphorically to convey that someone lacked stability, support, or a sense of belonging. It suggests that the person faced challenges or difficulties, perhaps feeling unsteady or without a secure position in life. The phrase can be found in literature and dreams, where chairs symbolise internal struggles and need. It's akin to declaring that someone didn't have a solid foundation or a place to rest comfortably.

Saturday 9th October

Oh, that we were out of this tropical heat it is like an oven, melting the marrow in the bones. Left my bed and spent the night on deck.

Sunday 10th October

Heat is terrific, too much for animal life. Captain read prayers in the saloon at 10.30 and in the evening a service was read in the third-class quarters. Two women fainted and a bullock was to kill on account of the heat. One of the women is very ill. Passengers had to leave their berths and were lying all over the deck, but this gave little relief as the midnight air was so hot we could hardly breathe.

Monday 11th October

Just sufficient clothing for decency. Yet the heat is almost like a furnace, Edith is very sick and poorly and has all the symptoms of a Tropical fever. A splendid Eastern sunset.

Tuesday 12th October

Thankful Edith is better. At 11.30 am we crossed the Line and are in the Eastern Hemisphere again. Killed two sheep and one bullock. Speed away Tuesday evenings and bring me better society for this is a prayless (sic) and Godless place.

On this day, the Line was crossed again, but John does not refer to any ceremony. As this was a passenger line, one would have thought that at least some reference to the ship crossing the Equator would have been mentioned.

Wednesday 13th October

Heat less oppressive, Edith and all other sick ones better. Expect to reach Aden on Sunday. This evening, we had another of those tropical and oriental panoramas which time will never blot from memory's page. Oh, that I had the power to describe the scene. The sun is setting in blood, his background a clear blue sky, his curtains pink, scarlet rose, magenta, crimson, amber, yellow and all the imaginable hues, while clouds like forest trees are piled on either side. The glorious galaxy of the stellar heavens "Worlds upon worlds amazing pomp" the sea like a sheet of glass. Flying fish in scores skating on the placid water, shoals of large porpoises gambolling near the ship's side, all fill my soul with a profound reverence for the great Creator and remind me of the majestic lines of Pollock:-

Whose garments were the clouds
Whose minstrels brooks, whose lamps the moon and stars,
Whose angel choirs the voice of many waters,
Whose bouquets, morning dews, whose heroes storms,
Whose warriors, mighty winds, whose lovers, flowers,
Whose orators, the thunderbolts of God,
Whose palaces, the everlasting hills,
Whose ceiling, heavens unfathomable blue.

John quotes lines from the fifth book of The Course of Time, a ten-volume poem in blank verse by the Scottish poet Robert Pollok, who lived from 1798 to 1827. This was the last published and most famous work of Pollok.

Thursday 14th October

A further diminution of the heat as we leave the Equator, but we may expect a recurrence in the Red Sea. A good wind and a pleasant sailing. A day's sail nearer home, what a joyful thought. Have just finished after three days reading the life of that noble man John Ashworth of Rochdale.

Having never heard of John Ashworth, JHH wrote to the Rochdale Libraries and Arts Services and was provided with the following information:

John Ashworth was born on 8 July 1813, the son of a woollen weaver. He became the minister at the Chapel for the Destitute, which he had founded after the suffering of the poor was revealed to him during a visit to London. As an author, pamphleteer, and traveller, he acquired a worldwide reputation and popularity, which remained with him until his death on 26 January 1875.

A.L. Calman wrote a biography of John Ashworth, "Life and Labours of John Ashworth," published in 1875. This was the edition that John had read.

Friday 15th October

A sea of glass, a bright blue sky, a burning sun, whales blowing up, flying and jelly fish in abundance, truly we are in the tropics. At 8 pm passed Cape Guardafin off the coast of Africa and in the moonlight had a good view of the rocky shore. Here some time ago 5 ships having gone too near the shore were plundered by the natives. Met two fishing smacks carrying bright lights.

Saturday 16th October

Fine but very sultry morning. Met and passed a ship at 8 am. Are now in the Gulf of Aden but as we don't require coal are not going to call there. The bright moonlight seems to inspire our passengers, for music, dancing and fencing by the Frenchmen was carried on to a late hour on deck.

Sunday 17th October

Scarcely a breath of air and the heat is worse than ever this morning. At 2 am passed Aden and at 10 am passed through Hells Gate or the Strait of Babel Mandeb having a good view of the coasts of Mocha Arabia on the right or Asiatic side and Abyssinia on the left or African side. An exciting time for after having seen only one ship in the Indian Ocean for three weeks, we met and passed in the Strait 4 steamers and 3 little boats with sails set. One of the latter had a lot of Africans on board in an almost nude state and from their savage looks I had no desire for any nearer acquaintance. At night the air was so hot the cabins below were like ovens and the deck was covered with people trying to sleep with only a covering over their faces to save them from moon blindness which in these parts is very dangerous. I managed to sleep 5 hours in a draught under a boat and Mamma and baby on the forecastle got little sleep.

These days moon blindness is associated with horses, but the Victorians believed that it could result from the moon shining in one's eyes while asleep.

Monday 18th October

Several ill of diarrhoea on account of the heat and no wonder, for the perspiration is running down our bodies although our dress is a near approach to that of our first parents. At 11 am the thermometer is 110 F in the shade. At 2 pm passed three steamers one of which was a fine large boat of the P & O line. This is the hottest night we have had, even the little air we are getting off the African coast is as hot as though coming out of a furnace.

Tuesday 19th October

We shall never forget the heat of the Red Sea. Our butcher says that six years ago he was coming this route on the S.S. Cusso when her machinery broke down and she was disabled. Prayers were offered up at port, and she was given up, however, she managed to reach London in 160 days by the use of her sails. Just about where we are now many of her passengers succumbed to the heat including 10 in the second saloon. One man requested the Captain that should he die, a good coffin be made for him as he had a horror of being thrown overboard in canvass and the remainder of his money being given to the Seaman's Widows and Orphans fund. At noon his body was found on the seat of the W. C. One gentleman feeling himself going passed his ring to a fellow passenger and in three days both occupied the same grave, the unfathomable deep. Am myself very poorly from the heat, it seems too much for my weak constitution. Evening killed a bullock and three sheep. Are opposite Mecca in Arabia on the right and Nubia our left.

Wednesday 20th October

A head wind but cooler than if coming off the coast on either side. At noon passed two steamers and at 4 pm passed two islands called the Twin Brothers. At 12 pm had a fine moonlight view of the coast on either side as we are entering the Gulf of Suez having just passed Desolation Islands on the left. The dangers of the Red Sea on account of the coral rocks are many. Oh, my Lord, on the coast of Egypt I this night consecrate myself to Thee and promise if Thou will guide me safely home that my life shall be fully devoted to Thee.

Thursday 21st October

Stood on deck until 2 am watching the towering rocks and a revolving light on the coast of Egypt. This light was put up by the P & O Company on a projecting rock where one of their steamers was wrecked. The scenery is splendid in the early morning as the Gulf gets narrower up to Suez. At 8 am we passed 4 steamers. The Irishman before mentioned had another fit on deck this morning. Our afflictions are never so great, but we see others who have greater, how thankful I am I never had a fit. I am looking into the sea for some of Pharaoh's chariot wheels as we must be very near the spot where the Lord took them off Pharaoh's chosen chariots of Egypt with which the Israelites were pursued. Got out my bible and as I sat on deck reading the history of that miraculous interposition, Exodus 14/15, with the place before my eyes readers judge what my feelings were. Perpendicular rocks 60/100 ft high and between them a plain of sand for about 50 yards, I could fancy God's chosen people standing in the aperture and lifting up their eyes over the sand desert behind them and seeing their enemies pursuing them turning upon the meek Moses and derisively saying "Because there were no graves in Egypt hast thou taken us away to die in the wilderness". And I could almost hear the hoary prophet saying "Fear ye not stand still and see the salvation of the Lord which He will show you today". Then stretching out the rod and dividing the waters and the sacramental host of God's elect passing through dry shod.

At 3 pm arrived at Suez and were immediately surrounded by about a dozen bumboats with Arabs and Gypsies displaying their wares, such as coral, shell necklaces, drink, apples, figs, pomegranates, salmon, sardines, tobacco, cigars, etc; they did a good stroke of business especially in the brandy. Their modus operandi was for one of the men from each boat to climb by a rope like a monkey up the side of a ship and draw his wares in a basket as called for. They have black or bronze skins, wear turbans and long cotton gowns with a belt around the waist, white stockings and sandals. They speak a broken English except when speaking to each other and ask four times the value of every article.

Suez is a little town about the size of Crook, the buildings looking clean and new. The pilot having boarded us at 4 pm we entered the Canal. The greatest attraction of this memorable day was the Arab boys, clad in Eden's luxury of dress viz; a rag to cover their nakedness, who ran by our side on the bank of the Canal for three of four miles crying "Backsheesh" money "Backsheesh". Biscuits, nuts, potatoes and coin were thrown them and, in their eagerness to catch them they plunged up to the chin and performed curious antics in the water to the amusement of the saloon and nabob passengers especially. As it is not safe to navigate the Canal at night, we anchored at 7 pm; in one of the sidings provided, for it is so narrow that ships cannot pass, and the night being warm and moonlight fishing and bathing went on until late.

JHH comments that "To a person of such deep religious conviction this must have been a most wonderful experience. John Hillary firmly believed in the Old Testament (and who is to say he was wrong to do so) and to be passing the places where these things took place undoubtedly moved him very deeply. It must have been exciting ...for the next day or so to see these biblical scenes passing before his eyes. Here was something to tell his class about on his return."

Friday 22nd October

Weighed anchor at 7 am but before starting a French Steamer passed us with hundreds of wretched dirty Arabs who cheered us in passing. Their dress was a turban and a gown of dirty blue print, and they were making the periodical pilgrimage to Mecca to perform the obligations of the Mahomedan religion, or rather delusion, for what more can it be which leaves its votaries so debased. Christianity raises men everywhere and, in every respect, but Mahomedanism (sic) leaves its disciples base in their morals, dark in their minds and filthy in their persons. The coasts of Arabia on the right and Egypt on the left are, as far as the eye can see, nothing but rock, sand and barrenness everywhere.

Suez Canal is 93 miles long, is cut through the land of Goshen and varies in width from 50 yards to 5 or 6 miles where it goes through two lakes. It is worked by telegraphic communication and sidings are provided at intervals for steamers to wait in passing. In the narrow places great care is needed and we only went about 4 miles per hour, but in the lakes about 10 miles. On the banks on either side small native hamlets are springing up with their flat roofed, sand or concrete built houses of one storey, some of which have small gardens and a few trees growing in them. Women are standing at the doors, at least such I took them to be, but their dress makes the sexes difficult to distinguish, children playing around, dogs lounging and goats grazing on the poor herbage on which only goats, donkeys and camels can subsist. One of these houses attracted attention particularly, standing on a small island with palm and other trees growing around it and fishing boats moored close by.

At 1 pm passed near Ishmaelia. A drove of about 200 camels and 2 ponies in charge of a few Arabs on the right and camels bearing burdens with an Arab trudging by their sides on the left hand. (Scripture scenes rise). It is not unusual for large steamers to ground in the Canal, have to discharge their cargo and be detained for days, however, we got through safely and reached Port Said about 10 pm. The town contains 3,000 inhabitants, Turks, Greeks, Arabs, Gypsies and Africans and has sprung up as an outcome of the Canal scheme. The people are low, cowardly, treacherous villains, living by barter, fraud and the wages of iniquity. Several of our male passengers went ashore for a night's debauch, but one of them told me on their return he felt sorry he had gone and witnessed such moral depravity.

The natives boarded our ship by scores displaying their wares in great variety and talking sanctimoniously of "Father Jacob" extorting as much from the passengers as they could and when money was done, change for change. The most amusing part of the affair was when a boat came alongside with a supply of water from the Nile, which empties itself here and 4 barges with 600 tons of coal. About 150 miserable wretches without shoes or stockings carried the coal in baskets on their shoulders and tipped them into the hold. All night long did their babble continue until few got any sleep. I suppose this was kept up to incite the idle scoundrels to work but two ganders fighting never made a greater row among a flock of geese and 50 Englishmen would have beaten them all for work. The coal was Welsh, being kept here to supply passing steamers.

This entry seems shocking to us today, but John was living at the height of the British Empire, and Britons did feel superior to all other peoples, especially non-whites. Britain had taken the lead in the Industrial Revolution, and this created an intense feeling of superiority that probably had some justification. It was even taught in schools. Here is John, a committed Christian, demonstrating this superior attitude by classifying the locals as wretches, villains, and scoundrels without even realising his hypocrisy.

Saturday 23rd October

Resumed our journey at 6 am and passing Alexandria with the pillar called the Pharos on our left, we were soon in European waters in the Mediterranean Sea. Weather fine with good Welsh coal, which is 50% better than colonial, making only half the ashes and twice the steam, we are ripping through the ocean at great speed. Being now in the track of vessels we saw several large ships and steamers during the day. These are dull Saturday nights and increase the longing for home, but I hope another will be the last on the sea. The temperature being now comfortable, I retired early to bed for rest and quiet thought, treacherous memory tantalized me with the remembrance of: -

Hopes that were angels in their birth

But perished soon like all of earth

A person on board from Scotland told me that he has been 21 years in Victoria and Gippsland but has had no home comforts. He says sunstroke is very common, the thermometer sometimes being 104 F. in the shade in harvest time, and those having sunstroke once are always after mentally dull. He says mature life is from 27 to 30 years after which decline soon follows, that girls marry usually at 15 and can be seen with one child by the hand and another at the breast, the mother looking only like a schoolgirl herself.

The poetic quotation is from Lord Byron's *Childe Harold's Pilgrimage*, an epic poem published in 1812 that brought Byron fame and literary renown. The phrase reflects disillusionment and longing that resonated with a British public tired of endless battles against Napoleon. But here, in John's case, he was doubtless thinking about the hopes and aspirations he had harboured on his outward journey, which were now dashed forever.

Sunday 24th October

Fine morning. Going at a rare speed. All thoroughly sick of the monotony of sea life and counting the days until we reach home. I am tired of the forced companionship of wicked men and meditating on the goodness of Him who led Joseph like a flock and has guided me my life long. Sacred as was the Temple to the Jews it had not more attractions than the old Chapel at home has for me, poor as it looks its hallowing influence does my heart good even now, both in the retrospect and the prospect. Although the Sabbath is to be observed as religiously as circumstances will permit, how this holy day is desecrated. Butcher washed out grain store, killed 2 sheep and 1 bullock and everything went on as on a weekday.

Monday 25th October

A rough sea, ship pitches heavily, several sick again. This evening the sky was dark, black clouds out of which lightning flashed ahead indicative of a coming storm. Everything moveable is lashed to the bulwarks and in a few minutes the storm is upon us. We had the electric light in reality the deck being flooded with light which quivered and lingered until the most stout-hearted were afraid. Killed 6 sheep today.

Tuesday 26th October

Very rough sea, white horses on each side after the storm last night truly we are "Rocked in the cradle of the deep" and all sickly. At 11 am 4 ships are in view and the coast of Italy discovering itself. What a pleasure to see European shores again. At 2 pm under the shelter of the coast the sea calm. A fine view of Reggio and some small villages, towering hills, creeks, vineyards and fruitful fields. Truly Italy is a land of beauty. But yet more beautiful still did some pronounce the coast of Sicily on our left with Messina in full view. At sunset we passed the Lipari Islands and Stromboli belching out its fire and smoke was so near that some of the children were afraid and asked if that was the place where all wicked people were to go. Am sorry Etna was too far away to descry plainly. The scenery of this day will never be forgotten by us.

Wednesday 27th October

Another memorable day. Before daybreak we reached Naples, the pride of Italy, and reputedly the prettiest city in the world. Had a splendid view of Vesuvius in the dawn casting up smoke, fire and lava from its crater and on the other side of us the city as seen from the bay is most picturesque, a perfect panorama. A railway train is drawn by a standing engine up the mountain side and quite a town of houses are clustered around its fertile base. Before anchor was cast scores of men and women were round us in their boats with baskets of fruit, wines and a variety of showy common jewellery. Several passengers went ashore and were fleeced of money and virtue. The streets of the city are narrow but very clean, being all paved and many having trees growing along their sides. The houses are generally five storeys high and very uniform. There are many fine public buildings and the whole standing upon rising ground is seen to advantage from the harbour. Resumed our voyage at 3 pm.

Thursday 28th October

Captain Groves being now running against time and steaming at full power we have got a good rocking during the night. The oscillation from the propellers is so very unpleasant, several again sick this morning. Sighted Sardinia at 11 am and passed opposite Cape Spartivento at 3 pm going 13 miles per hour. Sighted sometimes 4 ships at one time and so many during the day I did not think it necessary to mention them all separately. Of all the sights upon the sea that of a ship in full sail is the prettiest and landsmen can form no adequate conception of its beauty at a distance. When the ship is decked out in all her canvas and every sail swelled and careering gaily over the erratic waves, how lofty she looks, how gloriously her gallant course she goes, how she seems to lord it over the angry deep, moving apparently by her own volition and playing like a huge monster of the deep.

"She walks the water like a thing of life
And dares the angry elements to strife"

I cannot find the above lines directly attributed to any specific author. They do bear a resemblance to Coleridge's "The Rime of the Ancient Mariner" as well as to Byron's "She Walks in Beauty." We have seen that John was familiar with both works, and perhaps the beauty of a ship, about which he is waxing lyrical, has inspired him to compose his own poetic lines.

Friday 29th October

A rough sea which increased in severity as the day advanced and the afternoon is awfully tempestuous, seas breaking over us. The ship is almost standing still although her engines are working up to full power so strong is the wind and so high is the sea. Many passengers are looking alarmed "My fears are great, and my strength is small" Lord save us. I often doubt whether we shall reach home again.

Saturday 30th October

Weather still very rough and everything wet and uncomfortable. The Spanish coast on our right very plainly in view, also 17 ships sighted at one time and 30 during the day besides four steamers going the same course as us. These we passed nearly together opposite Cape de Gata about 4 pm. At 9 pm are opposite Malaga from whence a flashlight is shining brightly. A stormy night.

John is referring to Cabo de Gata, a large coastal area in Andalusia, which possesses a rugged landscape. It is the only region in Europe with a hot, desert landscape.

Sunday 31st October

Especially on Sabbath days do I feel most impatient to be away from the wicked practices and workers of iniquity. When I think of nearly 500 on this ship candidates for eternity how I feel for them yet all I can do is by my own example. My precepts only raise the jeers and scoffs of the wicked and are as pearls before swine, so I answer not a fool according to his folly. At 4 am was on deck and had a straight view of the Rock of Gibraltar as we passed through the strait. At 10 am we are steering out into the Atlantic and keeping towards the coast of Portugal. Evening another religious parody was attempted in our quarters but only about 6 attended. Tyler, our steward, who had been cursing during the morning took his stand and began to read a dangerously heterodox sermon of which he said the Rev. H.W. Beecher was the author. During the performance he was greeted with groans and cries "Remember the cheese you stole from the passengers yesterday". And a canful of hot coffee was poured from above on him. Bad as he was, I felt sorry for him. He abruptly desisted and walked from the stand, uttered a horrid curse against the sailors. Passed Cape St. Vincent at midnight.

Henry Ward Beecher was an American Congregationalist clergyman, social reformer, and speaker known for his support of the abolition of slavery and his emphasis on God's love. He was a strict teetotaller but, in 1875, had been involved in an adultery trial.

Monday 1st November

Strong head wind impedes progress. At 8 am are opposite Lisbon harbour and at 11.30 am opposite the Burlin Islands on our left. The day so much improved in the afternoon that the sea became like a lake and at 8 pm and up to midnight were going along sweetly at 14 miles per hour.

Tuesday 2nd November

About 2 am a great change in the weather took place and at 6 when I went on deck the wind and the rain were beating against us and the sea was in a very angry mood indeed. At noon the ship is rolling and pitching until we cannot stand, and many are poorly. Lord save us.

Wednesday 3rd November

In the Bay of Biscay again awful weather, a terrible day. God of mercy preserve us for my heart faints as the ponderous seas dash over our bows and make our noble ship tremble as a leaf and stop for the moment as though considering what to do. The angry billows are rising like mountains covered with white foam. Oh, the dangers of the deep.

Thursday 4th November

At 4 am passed the Lizard and at 8 Eddystone Lighthouse and at 10 arrived and anchored in Plymouth Sound. The sight of old England's shores sent a thrill of joy through the hearts alike of passengers and crew even the good old ship seeming to share in the general rejoicing:

"They may say what they will,
But no Englishman's heart,
What 'ere his condition may be,

But feels a keen pang,
When he's forced to depart,
And a thrill when he comes back to thee.
For whatever thy faults,
Thou art dear to us all,
No matter what strange countries boast,
No blessings are there,
That can ever compare,
With our home on thy sea girded coast.
Then here's to thyself,
Thou wee bonny land,
There's a bumper old England to thee,
Brave sons and fair daughters,
Shall join heart and hand,
And sing Ho for the land of the free".

At 11.30 weighed anchor and started up the Channel at the entrance of which we passed 81 ships and 14 boats. How spirited we all begin to feel, indeed the thought of home is a tonic both of body and mind.

Friday 5th November

Detained in the Channel by a fog and anchored in the evening about the Downs.

Saturday 6th November

Fog continues and our ship being so large and drawing so much water the pilot is afraid to venture, and we are still 10 miles below Gravesend. Wearisome delay but although disappointed at not getting home tonight it is the happiest of the last fifty.

Sunday 7th November

Weighed anchor at 7 am and proceeded up the Thames. Passed hundreds of ships of which one was the "Hooper" which I am told recently landed in one cargo 11,000 tons of grains from America to Liverpool. Arrived in the Royal Albert Dock, London at 5 pm, and proceeded via the Great Northern Railway, home.

So, John and his family are back on dry land after fifty-six days at sea. This was thirty-one days less than the journey aboard the "Westland", during which no stops were made.

On the return journey, several stops were made, although none were of long duration, and the journey was significantly shorter in distance due to its route through the Suez Canal.

JHH writes: Thus, at that time, the difference between steam and sail was insignificant if the latter were fortunate with the weather – we read of the "John Elder" doing 13 miles per hour. Under favourable conditions, sailing vessels could easily exceed that figure. As power increased, however, so did speed, and a modern vessel could maintain 25/30 miles per hour or three times the speed of the "John Elder".

Chapter 5
THE AFTERMATH

JHH ended his book with a chapter which he called Epilogue. In it, he recalled memories of his Hillary ancestors, some of which must have been passed down to him as families often do. He relates intimate and heartfelt tales of John and Elizabeth and their children, but, by his own admission, he was unaware of much about the family. He wrote, "It must be borne in mind that almost 100 years have elapsed, and all the actors have left the stage".

The Internet, genealogical websites, and some memories from my former wife, Elisabeth, have helped me discover much more information about the family, and I have included it in this final chapter as an enhancement to JHH's recollections.

Let us begin with John Hillary. He departed from Tow Law on Friday, 21st November 1879, having bid farewell to his mother and his many friends, including those of his "class". It must have been so disheartening for him to return just under a year, a day later than expected. He does not record his feelings or the events of that day. Still, one can only imagine his emotions on learning that his mother, Margaret, whom he referred to as "she who bore me and tenderly raised me from helplessness" when he left the previous year, had died very shortly after his departure to New Zealand.

Upon his return, he was given such a tremendous welcome, with people lining both sides of Station Street, that he said he "resolved to lay down his bones among them."

He went to his "class" the following Tuesday. JHH imagines that if so, "it must have been quite a night ...and on this occasion at least, Scriptures took a back seat".

Soon after his return, though, we know that John became a shopkeeper again. Being a prudent man with a keen eye for business, he may not have sold up when he left for New Zealand, and perhaps Thomas, his older brother, who he left behind, took charge of the shop in his absence. Thomas had worked with John from an early age.

We know that in later life, he owned several shops; besides groceries, he traded in new and second-hand furniture and household ironmongery.

JHH's father, "Baby Herbert", told him about an incident in the grocery shop that got him into serious trouble and disgrace. It seems that one day, while Herbert was in the store, John needed to get something high up, and to reach it, he was foolish enough to place one foot on a barrel of treacle. In those days, treacle was sold in barrels rather than in jars or tins as it is today. John's weight proved too much, and the end of the barrel broke, leaving John with one leg inside the barrel and the other outside it. As John was relatively small in stature, the accident may well have proved much more painful than his son imagined, and Herbert's "hoots of laughter" were not well received by his father. The shop had to be closed while John's leg was extricated from the barrel, and he put on a fresh pair of trousers.

Later, Herbert's father gave him a severe lecture. In Victorian times, it was just "not done" for children to laugh at a parent, and certainly not at John.

Another story involves the household ironmongery business rather than the grocery store. It centres around the first consignment of "centre draught lamps" that John received. Before the advent of electricity, the only form of lighting that the inhabitants of Tow Law used was oil lamps. These lamps typically had one or sometimes two flat wicks. The centre draught lamp boasted a circular wick that allowed air to be drawn through its middle, thus creating a much brighter light which, no doubt, caused much excitement throughout Tow Law.

John was keen to learn from his customers how well these new lamps were performing and, naively, he asked certain of them to take a lamp home to try and then to provide him with feedback. John and his wife, Elizabeth, even went out walking at night to where the customers lived, and the brightness emanating from some houses revealed where they were being used. Perhaps it wasn't surprising that the lamps were never returned. Nevertheless, John soon faced a tremendous demand and ended up selling the new lamps as quickly as he could get delivery.

On 16th June 1882, the family was blessed with another addition when Elizabeth gave birth to a baby daughter named Ethel Annie Hillary.

John continued to be a committed Wesleyan and a preacher. This meant that he spent many evenings and Sunday afternoons away from his home and family as he made his journeys into the surrounding districts, which could prove to be highly inhospitable in the dark winter months. John was keen to keep the Sabbath holy and, observing the rules in Deuteronomy 5: 12-15, which say that on it "you shall not do any work…or your ox or your donkey or any of your livestock", he refused to harness his pony into a trap and insisted on making all his journeys on foot.

So, on foot and in all weathers, John would set off with his bible in one hand and a storm lantern in the other. He would spurn the roads because he knew the countryside so well, especially the shortcuts. This was reasonable in fine weather, but it was quite a different matter when the snow began to fall in the fells. John's wife, Elizabeth, would become extremely worried on such occasions, and more than once, she would be in the process of organising a search party when suddenly John would emerge from the murk and show great surprise at all the fuss that was being made about him. This attitude was a great testament to his faith: God would protect him, and no mishaps did occur.

As a non-drinker, it was no surprise that John became involved in the temperance movement. John and his fellow workers had organised what they described as a "temperance lecture" and had a local bigwig as the main speaker. After John, as chairman, had introduced him, the bigwig took the floor and began to speak on the theme of "Purer Beer for the Working Man". This was not to the committee members' liking as they did not believe in drinking any beer, pure or otherwise. When the speaker had finished, John got up to close the meeting. He thanked the speaker but felt bound to add that the committee members could not agree with all he had said.

Afterwards, the speaker was keen to discuss his point with John, and it was explained to him that any form of alcohol was unacceptable. The speaker retaliated by saying he believed in temperance and had not been invited to talk about total abstinence. John had not been able to differentiate between these two terms.

The 1891 census describes John's occupation as "surveyor, ironmonger, and furniture broker," marking a departure from his previous life as a shopkeeper. He was an astute businessman, and JHH wondered whether, observing the rise of co-ops and multiple stores, he realised they would provide stiff competition to the local shop and decided it was time for him to branch out.

His life changed considerably when he began working for the local council. In addition to being a surveyor for the Tow Law Urban District Council, he was for several years a rate collector and secretary to the Tow Law Popular Building Society.

His work entailed a large amount of bookkeeping, and JHH writes, ".... this work he largely did at home in a small room known as the office. He did beautiful writing and figures, and these books were models of neatness. So particular was he that he always bought ink in penny bottles, half of which he always threw away, lest the ink get thick and cloudy, and at the same time, he fitted a new nib into his pen-no fountain pens or ballpoints in those days.

Now, it so happened that in the joke shops of the time, one could buy a joke consisting of a penny ink bottle and a large piece of shiny rubber that looked exactly like a huge ink blot. The bottle had only to be laid on its side, and the illusion was complete. My father purchased one of these, and when we next visited Tow Law, choosing a suitable opportunity by finding one of the account books open and grandfather absent, placed the joke in position while the rest of us awaited developments.

Soon, there was the sound of loud lamentations, and we all rushed into the office to see the fun. There was the old gentleman poking the blot with a piece of blotting paper, by which it refused to be absorbed; it was only when the blot began to move across the page, leaving a clean sheet, that the truth began to dawn. Thus did Herbert get a little of his own back for the treacle incident, though he had had to wait quite a few years."

I have discovered an extract from the Auckland Chronicle, which refers to a gathering in the Tow Law Wesleyan church on a Saturday evening in 1909 to celebrate John Hillary's fifty years as a local preacher. The celebration probably coincided with John's seventieth birthday.

The item states that "in order to give tangible expression to the esteem in which Mr. Hillary is held, his brother, Thomas, local preachers and numerous friends in the Weardale and Crook circuits subscribed to an English lever gold watch" which was handed to him at the occasion during which "interesting speeches and reminiscences were given, and the function throughout proved a very happy one."

John gave a speech, and although it touched upon his emigration to New Zealand, it was much more concerned with his life as a Methodist. His parents were Methodists, and they took him to the "House of God" at the age of seven. Coming out, they were met with a blinding snowstorm, and his father said, "You cannot see. Shut your eyes and put your hand in mine, and I will lead you home." John added that he had gone through various storms since then, but had always heard his Heavenly Father saying, "You cannot see the way, but I will lead you."

He told the gathering that he had begun preaching at the age of eighteen and a half and had delivered his first sermon at Frosterley, near Weardale. Since then, he had preached and lectured throughout the Weardale and Teesdale circuits, as well as in Barnard Castle, Bishop Auckland, Consett, Newcastle, and various other locations.

John told entertaining stories of his long journeys on dark winter nights, often returning home after midnight. He spoke of his trials, triumphs, and the happiness he found in his work. He finished by saying that the Methodist church was not only the church of his birth but also his choice, and the few remaining years of his life "should be entirely devoted to the Saviour to whom he owed his all."

TOW LAW LOCAL BOARD.

NOTICE.

Any person found depositing any Timber, Stone, Iron, Dung, Manure, Slops, or any other matter in the Channels or Street Traps, or upon the Streets or Highways within the Board District, will be prosecuted.

By order of the Board,

W. GARRAWAY, Inspector.
J. HILLARY, Surveyor.

Myles Taylor, Gas Printing Works, Hope Street, Crook.

Tow Law Local Board Notice

Some indication of John's role as a local council surveyor is shown in the above flyer. Whatever John's other responsibilities with the local council were, he was sufficiently exalted to be put in charge of organising Tow Law's celebration of King George V's coronation, which took place in Westminster Abbey on 22nd June 1911. John was given the role of walking across a field at dusk, torch in hand, and lighting a huge bonfire. JHH, who would have been seven at the time, remembers standing in the dark later with his father and some local worthies, looking across the Pennines, observing the other fires that could be seen from miles around.

THE AFTERMATH

This may well have been the last time that JHH saw his grandfather because in three years, he would be dead, and later that same year, Britain would be in the throes of the Great War.

John Hillary passed away at 7.15 a.m. on 23rd January 1914. His death certificate states that the cause of death was "senile decay", which means a decline or deterioration of physical strength or mental functioning, especially of short-term memory or alertness, because of old age or disease. His son, Herbert, was in attendance when he died.

Later, his Quarterly Ticket of Membership to the Wesleyan Methodist Church, reprinted below, was found inside his bible.

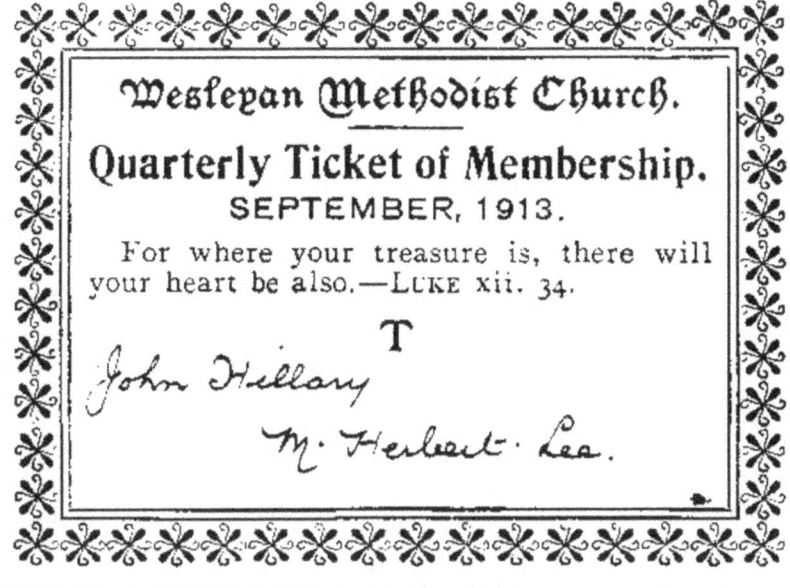

Wesleyan Methodist Church - Membership

But what of his wife, Elizabeth? I was disappointed that she received only a few mentions in the "Westland" journal. She was integral to the entire New Zealand venture, and with six young children to care for, including a baby in arms, her life aboard could not have been easy. It was good to read that John helped with the baby's washing at one point when Elizabeth was indisposed with seasickness. It was highly unusual for a father to undertake what was referred to as "woman's work" in these times.

Elizabeth Bainbridge was born on 12th September 1841 in Middridge, a small village in County Durham. Her father, Joseph, was a coal miner who later worked on the railways. The 1861 census describes his occupation as a railway platelayer.

A platelayer's job was to inspect and maintain the railway track, including all its components such as rails, sleepers, fishplates, and bolts. They also greased the points and generally monitored for wear and tear. The platelayers usually worked in gangs under the overall control of a foreman.

As the railway line development approached Tow Law, Joseph, presumably the foreman, chose the town as their headquarters and moved his family there.

The 1861 census lists their address as Dan's Castle, Wolsingham, and indicates that Joseph resides there with his wife, Margaret, and their two daughters, Elizabeth and Ann. Elizabeth, aged 19, earned her living as a dressmaker.

Also living in the same residence was a doctor, George Hood, a Scot, a general practitioner. More about him later.

The Bainbridge family played a crucial role in the burgeoning development of the railway. Other family members were responsible for the construction of the line from Darlington to York, which was regarded as one of the country's best examples of track engineering. In this case, an uncle was in charge of construction, and a nephew was in charge of surveying.

An uncle of Elizabeth, whose name was M. Bainbridge, was, according to JHH, the first railway guard in the world to be killed and possibly the first public railway employee to lose his life while on duty.

The early first-class carriages were little better than stagecoaches, fitted with iron wheels, and carrying luggage on the roof. It was part of the guard's duty to make sure that the luggage was safe, and while he was on the roof checking, he forgot that there was a tunnel at Shildon, and his head struck the parapet, killing him instantly.

With so much railway activity taking place in Tow Law, the construction gangs arriving with money in their pockets, and the Irish labourers from the coke ovens over the fells resenting the intrusion of the newcomers, at times, Tow Law turned into a Wild West town. With William Hillary as colliery manager and Joseph Bainbridge a man of some importance, it was inevitable that the families would meet.

Thus, John Hillary met and married Elizabeth Bainbridge.

Elizabeth took an interest in her husband's affairs and was of considerable help to him in running the shops. However, although she did not share his religious enthusiasm, she was a kind-hearted person who performed many good deeds and was always willing to help when needed. Although she suffered from seasickness aboard the "Westland", she subsequently never had any illness, not even a headache. Therefore, she seldom gave any sympathy to such sufferers.

Earlier, I mentioned Doctor George Hood, who lived with Elizabeth and her family in her late teens. In time, he became Tow Law's local doctor. There was a time when the town was stricken with an outbreak of smallpox.

Smallpox was a killer, with the chances of recovery being no higher than fifty/fifty. People were dying in their scores. Elizabeth soon realised that with overwork and lack of sleep, the doctor was almost out on his feet. So, she volunteered to help him. She became his unpaid nurse and assistant. Amazingly, neither she nor the doctor was affected by the disease.

One day, on her rounds, she heard singing coming from one of the houses and, aware that the sole occupant was an old lady who was dying, she went to investigate only to find the doctor sitting on her bed with his arms around her, giving his rendition of "Safe in the arms of Jesus". The old lady, who knew she was dying and was aware that there was nothing more that the doctor could do for her, requested that he sing her a hymn. He sang the only one he knew.

The two's friendship lasted many years. The doctor, being unmarried, moved in with Elizabeth and John and ran his surgery from their house. Elizabeth assisted him with his bills, which were never sent to the poor, but the amounts were increased for those who could afford to pay.

When the doctor died, the whole town turned out to see the cortege pass.

After John died in 1914, and with the advent of World War I, Elizabeth spent her time knitting socks for soldiers. She set herself a target of a pair per day.

In her final years, Elizabeth spent much of her time visiting relatives and friends, and she also spent long periods at JHH's home. She continued to make garments for her many children, and JHH says that he remembers the sound of the old treadle sewing machine in use until midnight and even after.

In January 1923, she set off for home from JHH's house. On the way, she called in on her sister in Shildon but never managed to return to Tow Law. She was taken ill and died there on 25th January.

Let us now look at what happened to John and Elizabeth's children.

William Arthur Hillary was the oldest, born on 21st April 1862 at Tow Law. The family always called him Willie. He was a humourist with a ready wit.

When the family returned to England from New Zealand, Willie, then seventeen years old, briefly worked as a stonemason in the local coal mine.

However, he soon became attracted to the Salvation Army. JHH explains that although his father was an ardent Wesleyan, his children were all very musical. Willie was an accomplished player on a Wheatstone concertina and a fine singer. He even had a knack for getting on with animals!

Being of a happy disposition, Willie much preferred the Salvation Army's livelier and jollier attitude rather than the "fire and brimstone" approach preached in the chapels and churches.

THE AFTERMATH

In 1879, the first Salvation Army brass band was established in Consett, approximately ten miles from Tow Law. I wonder if Willie and his brother John Tom went there to witness performances and, if so, to what extent it influenced them to join the Army.

Due to his religious background, Willie never considered a career on the stage, but JHH believed he was a natural showman. Perhaps he thought that a life in the Salvation Army accommodated this need in his personality. It was not only the religious aspect that appealed to him, as it also provided an outlet for his natural ability to attract people.

Willie met and married Mary Wrigley, who was also in the Army. She had been born in Oldham, Lancashire, and was a fine singer. The two of them would attend meetings singing solos and duets, and at the end, people would be encouraged to throw pennies onto their drum. This proved to be an excellent source of revenue and a means of recruiting new soldiers. A song like "The Bible my Mother gave to me" would produce a shower of coins.

Willie and Mary had two children, Albert and Florence, and both travelled with the Salvation Army.

But as Willie approached the age of fifty, his health began to deteriorate, and he spent the last months of his life suffering from paraplegia and then cystitis. In the end, he went into a uraemic coma, which lasted for three days before he died in Kentish Town, London, on 6th December 1912. It was a tragic demise for somebody who had devoted most of his life to the spiritual well-being of others.

I now turn to John Thomas Hillary, his younger brother, who was born on 20th January 1864. Upon his return to England, like Willie, he went to work in the colliery as a stone mason's apprentice, and like Willie, he joined the Salvation Army at an early age. By the time he was twenty-seven, he was an officer and a preacher, having decided that this was where his career lay.

On 29th August 1892, he married Fanny Barrett, who was also a member of the Salvation Army. She had toured the country with him, preaching at the various Army Citadels, and both had achieved an excellent reputation. John Tom and Willie were highly competent public speakers. The marriage ceremony took place at the Congress Hall in Plymouth and was performed according to the rites of the Salvation Army.

John Tom soon rose to the exalted rank of colonel and was always referred to as the "Colonel" by the Hillary family. He and Fanny had five children: Dorothy, Edith, Luther, Kathleen, and Muriel.

During his service with the Salvation Army, John Tom commanded several important divisions. For eight years, he held the post of the National Young People's Secretary, during which time he made significant advances in the work among young people. He had a remarkable organisational skill.

In September 1921, John was appointed Territorial Commander of all activities in the West Indies, which encompassed British Honduras, Cuba, Panama, the Canal Zone, Costa Rica, the Dominican Republic, and British Guiana.

With his wife and children, he sailed to Kingston, Jamaica, where the headquarters were based. Unfortunately, John, now in his late fifties, found it extremely difficult to cope with the oppressive heat, and after a stay of almost two years, he and his family returned to England.

His subsequent illness necessitated his retirement from the Army at the age of seventy-five, but he went on to fully recover and turned his attention to many other projects, including one involving leaving religious texts in London Underground trains.

His wife predeceased him in 1947. John died, aged ninety, on 13th May 1954 in Bromley, Kent.

Albert Ernest Hillary, the third brother, was born on 21st January 1868, and he embarked on a very different career path from Willie and John Tom. At thirteen, he was working as a coke oven plasterer.

Coke ovens are usually brick or other heat-resistant chambers that heat coal to separate the coal gas, coal water, and tar. The coal, gas, and water fuse with carbon and the remaining ash to form coke, a hard residue used primarily to produce iron and steel. The role of the plasterer is to apply a mixture of loam – a combination of clay and coke dust – into the tiny spaces between the bricks and the oven door, thereby diminishing and finally sealing off the air supply. It was an unhealthy and unsafe way to earn a living.

It is not surprising that Albert soon changed his occupation. By 1891, he had become a grocer's assistant, and ten years later, he had moved to Lanarkshire, Scotland, to run a confectionery manufacturing business — Carson's Chocolates. He was eventually appointed managing director. Carson's Milk Chocolate Cubes proved highly popular, and the expansion resulted in him selling the business to another company.

In December 1897, Albert married Annie Bartleet, and the couple went on to have three children: John, Constance and Mabel.

After the Great War, he bought a firm that had previously imported continental chocolate and confectionery machinery. His previous knowledge of the trade placed him in good standing.

In 1922, Albert stood as the Liberal candidate for Harwich, Essex, and won the seat by a majority of 764 votes. He held the seat in the 1923 general election but lost it to the Conservatives in 1924, as the Liberal Party was in national decline by this time.

For some time, he lived at Ardleigh, near Colchester in Essex. Upon his retirement, he moved to Royston, Frinton-on-Sea, also in Essex, where he died on 10th February 1954, at the age of 86.

Now we come to the first daughter, Edith Louise Hillary, born in Tow Law on 10th January 1874. In June 1900, she married Samuel Taylor, a Welshman from Monmouthshire. Although he was a sometime Evangelical preacher, his primary occupation was as a wholesale confectioner, at which he was highly successful. The couple had two daughters, Madge and Corie, and for many years, the family lived in Porth in the Rhondda.

Unfortunately, in later years, Edith succumbed to a serious illness, which led to her losing the use of her legs. She died in Whitchurch, Cardiff, on 20th January 1931 at 57, leaving Samuel a widower. Her death certificate states that she died from heart failure, but it adds that she suffered from "disseminated sclerosis", which we would refer to today as multiple sclerosis. Samuel died in 1940.

Next in line is Frederick Charles Hillary, who was born in Tow Law on 22nd August 1876. In his early years, he worked as a grocer's assistant, but his true passion was photography. At one time, he became the sole professional photographer based in Tow Law. In 1904, in the Wesleyan Chapel, he married a local lady called Alice Dixon. The couple had two children: Horace, born in 1905, and Mary, born in 1908. Horace became the father of my ex-wife, Elisabeth.

Frederick became a commercial traveller for Carson's Chocolates. He moved with his young family to Partick, Scotland, where the company was based and his older brother, Albert, had once been involved.

At the outbreak of the Great War, Frederick served in the Army Veterinary Corps, attaining the rank of corporal. He eventually saw action at Le Havre. At the end of the War, he and Alice moved to Ilford in Essex, where he became the London sales manager for Carsons.

As we shall see later, JHH's family also moved down from the north to Ilford, and he soon became friendly with his cousin Horace and his Uncle Fred. The three of them soon began spending much of their leisure time indulging in photography, cycling, and listening to the radio.

It must have been wonderful for JHH and Horace to have someone on hand like Frederick, who was able to instil his love of photography into them. JHH writes that he and Horace would "sally forth with a plate camera, a set of loaded plate slides and a folding wooden tripod, all of which were bulky and heavy. Thus, equipped, we would wander through the local parks and countryside in search of suitable subjects. On returning, we would lose ourselves in the cellar which, having no window, made an excellent darkroom and, there, with the aid of a red lamp and suitable trays, we would proceed to develop the results of our labours."

THE AFTERMATH

Another passion was radio, which was then known as wireless and was very much in its infancy. The early radio amateurs were sometimes referred to as experimenters. This stemmed from the fact that the Wireless Telegraphy Act of 1904 required anyone wishing to use wireless telegraphy for experimental purposes to apply for a licence from the General Post Office (GPO). Applicants were required to provide evidence of British nationality and a few character references. JHH and his uncle Fred managed to obtain their experimenters' licences.

There were no regular broadcasts and, of course, no BBC. Wireless aficionados would construct their own sets from parts purchased from wireless shops and use an outdoor aerial to send and receive transmissions. This would usually be a high pole erected in the garden.

JHH refers to the time when he and Frederick attempted to pick up an experimental transmission in the morning. If they could, they would almost certainly be able to tune into a very special programme they wanted to hear in the evening. He writes: "My uncle decided to check that his set was working. It was just as well, as there wasn't a sound from it. The valves glowed brightly, everything seemed in order, but nothing emerged. We then proceeded to take everything to pieces and spent a long time on it, but in the end, we were left with what looked like several cigar boxes with light bulbs on top and still nothing. It was at this point that my Aunt came in and informed my Uncle that she had removed the aerial lead-in wire because her washing was blowing up against it. At this point, I decided it was time for me to have an urgent appointment elsewhere and made a hurried departure."

By 1920, Frederick and his family had moved to Bristol, where he became the sales manager of the chocolate manufacturers. Unfortunately, his health began to fail him, and on 31st May 1929, he died at his home of chronic nephritis—an inflammation of the kidneys that, over time, led to their failure.

Finally, we come to the youngest family member to travel to New Zealand: Herbert Bainbridge Hillary, born on 13 February

THE AFTERMATH

1879, just before the voyage began. JHH admits that as Herbert was his father, he should be the person about whom he knows the most, but he adds that "of his earlier years I have only vicarious knowledge," and there is good reason for this.

I have discovered that, of all the siblings, Herbert seems to have had the unhappiest life. There is barely a mention of the religion that sustained and brought joy and fulfilment to his parents and brothers, and there is a lot of bad luck and bitterness.

Herbert was educated at Wolsingham Grammar School, and upon leaving, he served an apprenticeship in painting and decorating, which earned him his Master's Painting certificate. This designation indicated that the holder had demonstrated a level of craftsmanship and professionalism that set them apart from many others.

JHH relates that at the beginning of his adult life, it was customary for a man to learn a trade. The reason was that, should he later fall on hard times, he would always have something to turn back to.

Herbert's apprenticeship lasted seven years, and if this seems like a long time for someone to learn how to be a painter and decorator, JHH points out that "there were no ready-made paints, and a man had to mix his own for each job and know what colours to use. He had to push his trestles and ladders, etc., on a handcart, and as each job might be several miles away, in a very hilly district, this could be hard work. Wages were paid from the very time of the arrival at the job; time taken to get there and back did not count, and at the end of the day, you mixed your paints, etc., ready for the next morning."

At the time of the 1891 census, Herbert was twelve and still at school, which was unusual as the normal leaving age was ten. It was not until 1893 that the Elementary Education Act raised the age to eleven. So, we can assume that he was on the cusp of starting his seven-year apprenticeship, as by the time he was twenty-one in 1901, he was described as a journeyman painter.

But just as his career was getting underway, his life changed dramatically. On 5th February that year, he married Elizabeth Hodgson at the Weardale Register Office in Wolsingham.

This was a departure from the Hillary family's usual choice of the Wesleyan Chapel, but there was a good reason for this venue. On the same day the marriage occurred, Elizabeth gave birth to their first child—a daughter whom they named Maude. However, as a gesture of respectability, the birthdate was amended to the following day!

The couple had another child the following year, a boy who was named Leslie, but he died within a year of his birth.

Then, Herbert's business failed for reasons beyond his control, and he became bitter about its forced closure. The reasons were that many of the colliers were out of work and would take on decorating jobs cheaply, where they needed no special tackle. This left only the more difficult jobs for firms like Herbert's, such as painting staircases. So, he decided to close his business, and, with his family, he moved to Partick, Lanarkshire, to become the office manager of a wallpaper firm. JHH was born here in 1904.

Around 1910, Herbert changed jobs again, becoming a commercial traveller for a company based in Manchester called Baxendale & Co. They were a well-established firm of hardware manufacturers and suppliers of a vast range of products, including those for the decorating trade. Herbert's specialised knowledge stood him in good stead, and he remained with the firm for many years, travelling all over Britain, all week and only returning at weekends to see his family, who had now moved to Lancashire.

When the 1914-1918 War broke out, Herbert declared himself a conscientious objector, but he had to carry out work of national importance as a labourer at British Dyes in Huddersfield.

He also had almost no sight in one eye, which in any case would have precluded any active service. When the Armistice was signed on 11th November 1918, he did not bother to collect any wages and immediately returned to his old job at Baxendale.

Herbert's brother Albert asked him to come to London to work with him in the chocolate and confectionery machinery trade. The family then moved to Ilford, Essex.

Around 1930, Herbert grew restless and decided to work on his own account, feeling that he could work better for himself. By this time, his son, Haddon Hillary, was in his early twenties, and he was persuaded to join his father. After a few years, however, and with the approach of another war, which was creating an arms race on the Continent, importers began to find life increasingly difficult; Herbert was forced to close his business.

This was also a sad time because, in 1934, Herbert's wife, Elizabeth, died of cancer.

In 1938, Herbert remarried. His new wife was Florence Moseley, who came from Birmingham. The couple moved there, and Herbert lived in semi-retirement, working as a commercial traveller in the baking and confectionery trade.

On 4th February 1951, he died in hospital of bronchopneumonia at the age of seventy-two.

From left to right: Elizabeth, Maude, Herbert and JHH

Because Ethel was born in June 1882, long after the Hillary family had returned from New Zealand, JHH only grants her a passing mention in his book, which is primarily due to her status as his aunt "twice over".

This occurred because while his mother, Elizabeth Hodgson, married his father, Herbert, her brother George married Ethel. Thus, a brother married a sister, and a sister married a brother.

I have carried out some research and can add a little more information about Ethel. She was born on 16th June 1882, in Tow Law, and the 1901 Census shows that she was employed as a mother's domestic help.

In 1905, she married George Hodgson, a coal miner, in the Wesleyan Chapel, Tow Law. The couple had two children: Oswald and Winifred.

Ethel died on 26th July 1957 at 3 Whittington St., Doncaster.

Chapter 6
SUMMING UP

JHH concluded his book, first published in 1979, by stating that the Tow Law saga should now be at an end, as the Hillary family no longer had any association with the town. The main protagonists were all dead now and were not even buried in Tow Law. But he then adds that his unmarried sister, Maude, finding herself alone, had decided to move back and was living in a "splendid old people's home where she has a self-contained flat with all mod. cons".

However, my research reveals that Maude passed away in 1994, and as she was unmarried, that final link has gone. I would have enjoyed going to Tow Law, a place I'd never heard of before reading the book and perhaps seeing a grocery store bearing the name Hillary, attending a service at the Wesleyan chapel with members of the Hillary family forming part of the congregation, or going into the Black Lion pub and discovering that somebody with the surname Hillary drank there sometimes.

But we live in much different times now. I doubt whether the people living in Tow Law now have any knowledge of the Hillary family and their epic journey to New Zealand, the despair and frustration they encountered upon their arrival, and their unexpected return when the whole of Tow Law came out to welcome them home.

John Hillary was a man of firm conviction, sustained by his belief, who decided what he thought was best for his family. It did not work out, but John was not daunted. He made a successful life for himself when he returned to Tow Law, and his children, apart from poor Herbert, who was fortunate to have survived the outward journey, generally enjoyed successful and fulfilling lives.

So, accepting that Tow Law may have no further association with the Hillary's, my thoughts turned to New Zealand. I was intrigued by JHH's comments that in later years, some members of the Hillary family criticised John for "returning so quickly and not staying and facing the position," adding that he was fortunate to have access to sufficient money to pay for the return of his whole family.

I began to imagine what sort of dynasty would have been established had John and his family remained and "stuck it out". We'll never know. However, I also remembered JHH's words that John left a brother behind "who may have looked after his interests, and who we know later himself emigrated to, of all places, New Zealand."

This brother was Thomas Hillary, three years older than John and married to Ann Collinson. There is no further mention of Thomas in this context, and I had wondered if he had made his life successful in New Zealand.

Unfortunately, from what I can see on genealogical sites, if Thomas did emigrate, he did not remain in New Zealand for long, as he appears to have spent his later years working as a greengrocer in Durham, where he died at the age of eighty-four in 1920.

PHOTOGRAPHS

John Hillary

John Haddon Hillary

A page from John Hillary's diary

The Hillary family pew and commemorative plaque inside the Wesleyan Chapel at Tow Law

John Hillary's Golden Wedding – 17th June 1911

www.ingramcontent.com/pod-product-compliance
Lightning Source LLC
LaVergne TN
LVHW011208080426
835508LV00007B/666